THE
DIVINE
RESET

INCLUDES GROUP DISCUSSION AND JOURNALING GUIDE

Jarrod Cooper

Unless indicated, Scripture quotations are taken from The Holy Bible, New International Version®,
NIV®, Copyright © 1973, 1978, 1984, 2011 by Biblica, Inc. ®
Used by permission. All rights reserved worldwide.

Graphic Design by Victoria Cooper
Images from Canva

ISBN: 9798596764390

OTHER BOOKS BY JARROD COOPER
The Multisite Church Adventure
The Leadership Quest: Volume 1
Believe & Confess: Group Discussion Guide
500: Are we at the dawn of a new era in Glory?
Stronger: Building a powerful interior world
When Spirit & Word Collide
Glory in the Church

CHAPTERS

How to use this book

There are several ways to enjoy this book. You could of course simply read it, but if you want to go more deeply into the life-changing topics it highlights, you may want to consider:

The Divine Reset as a Journaling Guide (Paperback only)

The Divine Reset is written as a combination of prophetic insight, teaching and personal testimony, but the paperback version is also designed as a journaling tool, with space to respond to questions and discussion points as you take time to pray and reposition your own life or leadership for the future.

The Divine Reset as a 10 Session Group Discussion Course (all versions)

You could also use The Divine Reset as a discussion guide for your leadership team or small group. At the end of chapters 5-14 you will find in-depth questions, set across 10 sessions, to help your group discuss the prophetic themes outlined in the book. Have each group member read chapters 1-4 as an introduction, then read a chapter a week and gather to discuss, plan and pray.

Discounts for bulk purchases for use with small groups/teams are available from www.JarrodCooper.net

Introduction

Blearily I woke on the 9th September 2019, brushing away the duvet with the vivid memory of the night's dreams etched on my mind. I had had not one, but two vivid dreams from God that night and proceeded to scribble the headlines of what I had seen in my prophetic journal before the day began.

In the first dream I was wearing a watch, something I don't normally do. At some point in the night-time vision the little square that presented the date protruded from the watch face, blocking the hands from turning. It was a short dream, but very intense.

"A Pause!" I mused in my diary.

My second dream had followed a similar theme. In it I was walking the streets in the daytime, but it was dark, as if the sun had been delayed, time had been paused and the world was stuck waiting for the sun to rise.

Were these dreams a prophetic hint at some delay that was soon to come?

I noted the dreams in my journal and thought little of it. I, of course, had no idea that a "Great Pause" was about to erupt across the face of the entire planet, as a global pandemic was soon to sweep our world.

A few months later, on the 18th January 2020, we gathered around 150 of our church leaders in a hotel and invited proven prophetic minister and friend Dr. Sharon Stone to prophecy personally and corporately to us, hoping to align ourselves as closely to God for the coming season as possible.

I had for some time felt that 2020 marked more than a new season for us as a church and many others beyond. My prophetic feeling was that a whole new era was soon to engulf the earth, something I had written about extensively in my 2017 book *"500: Are we at the dawn of a new era of glory?"* But would Dr. Stone pick up on this theme and help us negotiate the coming changes?

Part way through our prophetic day with Dr. Stone, whose ministry we have enjoyed and proven for over 20 years, she began to prophesy about a new era coming and how we might position ourselves to enter it. This was a great confirmation!

But then she uttered, almost as a throw away comment, a phrase that now resounds like a trumpet in my soul:

"A new era is coming, but first there will be a short pause." There it was again, *"a Pause"*.

If I'm honest, I still thought very little of it. I guess I was about as wise to the meaning at that time, as the early disciples would have been to the significance of the minor prophets writings on the Day of Pentecost! Sometimes prophecy is only fully grasped during, or even after the event it is speaking about! It is only then that the words appear clearly enough for us to truly say, like Peter at Pentecost *"Ah! This is that, spoken by the prophet Joel."* (Acts 2:16).

But whether we grasped it or not, a pause was indeed about to befall the world.

Five months earlier, in August 2019, the U.S. prophet Chuck Pierce had apparently felt, during an annual prophetic retreat, that God was speaking of Passover 2020 as a time when we would be having a "real Passover" - that plague-like conditions would be affecting many around the world.(1)

As the pandemic burst upon the scene early in 2020, many nations would indeed find their peak of deaths and infections initially summit at around the 8-16 April, the time of that years Passover. While peaks and troughs, second waves and continuing grief has surged on for many months in many nations, the key point to Chuck's word seemed accurate enough for the part of the world where I live. During April 2020 we were indeed in the grip of a pandemic.

By the British spring of 2020 these three prophetic images above had fully converged as the COVID-19 plague led to waves of national lockdowns, empty church buildings, deserted streets, soaring unemployment and widespread economic downturn. The Great Pause had begun.

The Pit-Stop

On Tuesday 10th March 2020 as the United Kingdom was slowly gearing itself towards its first full lockdown, I had a vision during a staff prayer meeting.

In the vision a racing vehicle came to a pit-stop and an old wheel was removed from the automobile, to be replaced by a new Formula One tyre.

In my journal I later noted, *"A Pause, to update, that will result in acceleration."*

In my scribbles I continued, ruminating over a thought based on 1 Kings 18:46 where Elijah prepared himself for a new release of literal acceleration. *"When Elijah was about to outrun the chariot, he first tidied up his mantle – then the power of God came!"*

Elijah had a pit-stop moment to prepare for what was to come. He had to pause to tidy up his clothes before he ran. Was it time that I too, and perhaps many others alongside, should pause and prepare for this new era prophesied by God's messengers?

The visions, dreams and words recounted above have provided so much direction, usefulness and comfort to me in this strange 2020 year. They have propelled me into a season of soul searching, God seeking and realigning, asking some of the deepest, most profound questions of myself, my team and God Himself. A Great Pause has been thrust upon many of us, and the question of this book is, *have we all fully appreciated what God has been trying to say in this season?* Have we "changed our tyres" in God's divine pit-stop, or are we just desperate to get back to normal, happy to rush forward into the new era with the same old worn-out tyres on?

The promise in the pit-stop vision was that *"The Pause would lead to great acceleration"*, something I will come back to in far more detail later on. For now take a moment to ponder this initial, simple revelation…

This Pause has a Purpose

While I do not believe God has sent COVID-19 upon the world, or created the political responses that have followed, I do believe He is using this season as a deep challenge to our overly-busy lives and churches, allowing us time to tidy up our egos, our exhaustion and correct any mission-drift, making us ready for His new purposes.

He has prophetically warned us of this pandemic and promised us a pit-stop, all in the context of the birthing of a new era. And He is also promising acceleration to those who co-operate!

It is time, despite all the distraction of lockdowns, guidelines, headlines and slogans, that we go beyond the distracting info-demic that swirls blizzard-like around us, to enter the quiet rooms of God's restoration, preparation and wisdom, to discover where He is leading us, as we step beyond this most unusual of years.

As church members are we simply longing to go "back to normal" when God actually wants to lead us to a "new normal"? I know many hate that phrase, but that's often our grief talking. The braver part of each of us must reach deeper and ask – *"What is God saying to me in this time of preparation?"*

As church leaders have we also simply been in a rush to get "back to normal" as soon as we're able, or could this be a time for a revolution in our church life? Is it time for a cleansing, a resetting, a revival? Could this be a springboard for greater fruitfulness, harvest and transformation? Let us not miss this opportunity.

A Divine Reset

The essence of the book you hold in your hands, is the belief that this short pause, this ordained pit-stop time, is something God will use to perform a Divine Reset in the Church, ready for a new era ahead.

Dictionary.com states that the word "reset" means:

- to set again: to reset an alarm clock; to reset a broken bone.
- to set, adjust, or fix in a new or different way: to reset priorities; to reset prices.

Thesaurus.com gives us the synonyms of reset as *"reconstituted, reconstructed, transformed, altered, amended, corrected, improved, rectified, re-established, regenerated, renewed, reorganized, revised, revolutionized, reworked."*

Away from the stormy plains of a virus ravaged, fearful and panicked world, I believe the Church has been gifted a life-changing opportunity to pause and climb the mountain of God, to be transformed by His grace, to pause and ponder, to ask God to rework us ready for revolution, to prepare us perhaps even for a revival. I believe we would be fools not to fully utilise this pit-stop for a time of major reinvention and reorganisation, personally as individuals, locally as churches and globally as Kingdom influencers.

Perhaps you are reading this book many years from 2020, and you wonder if the challenges thoughts and provocations in this book have passed you by and the day for them is gone – but fear not, read on! Let's believe that in God's divine provenance now is your time for the pit-stop within these pages, and more importantly, that the journaling and prayers that follow, will lead you to a Reset in your own life.

The Prophets Are Speaking

Through the early lockdown weeks from March 2020 onwards, I began to broadcast nightly on several online platforms with worship, teaching and prophetic ministry, and this culminated in two weeks when I interviewed around fifteen key prophets around the world, as we tried to make sense of what God had been saying in this enigmatic season of pausing.

Prophets from the UK, USA, South Africa and Australia all aligned extraordinarily again and again, agreeing that this was a remarkable time of God's wisdom, and the wisdom from those broadcasts is a lot of what makes up this book. Around 50,000 viewed our Tribe TV broadcasts at the time, with thousands more since, as the obvious hunger for people to know what God is saying drew many to watch, listen and share.[2]

If we are to make the most of this divine pause, then we must know what God is saying about this recess and reset. What is its purpose, how we should respond, and how we can lead our churches and families beyond this time, into a prophesied new age?

I pray that as you read and ponder the questions placed at strategic points throughout the book, that your heart, and all those you lead and care for, would be moved by the presence of Jesus. I pray that you would embrace God's pit stop, and that the Holy Spirit would whisper of new adventures, new ways of living and new ways of transforming the world where you are. That the Father would engulf you in His love, and you would know deeply, profoundly, that this season has by no means surprised God, and He has your life, your family and your future in the palms of His powerful hands.

Jarrod Cooper
December 2020

Sources

1. Chuck Pierce Passover prophecy https://www.youtube.com/watch?v=9w-5ulM2_98&t=465s
2. The Prophets Speak - https://youtube.com/playlist?list=PL79_9Hj76zeJCEJbnxxbG-caljEzxOpk5

PART 1

DISCERNING THE TIMES

Chapter 1
"What Was That All About?"

"Nothing in life is to be feared; it is only to be understood. Now is the time to understand more, so that we may fear less." — Marie Curie

Right at the outset of our time together, I want to set a few thoughts in place regarding the 2020 pandemic and the ensuing political response in many nations. In the main this book is not actually about the pandemic or its aftermath, but rather about God's prophetic word to believers more broadly, and how He wants to bring transformation to our lives and usher in the next phase of His plans for us. But first I feel it would be wise to share a few prophetic thoughts God has given me about the pandemic for context, before we move on.

On 25th March 2020, as we were entering our first national lockdown in Britain, I spent time in prayer and was impacted by a vision of God's throne, standing strong over a dark ocean of fearful global events.

Immediately I was led to the verse:

"The LORD sits enthroned over the flood; the LORD is enthroned as King forever." Psalm 29:10

Upon seeing this vision and linking it to the verse in Psalm 29, I found that the Passion Translation of the Bible states in its notes that this verse speaks of the fact that God *"rules even over the dark flood of evil, to make it end"* – reassuring us that there is no season where He is not able to bring evil to an end and for goodness and mercy to triumph. This will be true of the events of 2020 and beyond. (1a)

I wrote in a prophetic blog at the time, *"Even now I am reign-*

ing over the flood of sickness, fear and sorrow moving over the face of the earth, to bring it to an end. I Am the God who "changes times and seasons" (Daniel 2:21) and even every evil thing remains under my control. As you cry out to me and call to me, I will answer."

I went on "This evil will end sooner than many claim. Though some will grieve as they are touched by personal sorrow, to many others this will be remembered as a time where you asked "What was all that about?!" – a time where fear and panic attempted to take over the hearts of men. But see, I Am enthroned above the flood to bring the evil to an end. Worship me, pray, seek my hand. Do not engage in the currency of fear that fills screens and newspapers. Do not be shaken. I decree "This shall pass!" – the times are set by my own authority."(2a)

"What Was That All About?!"

When you share a prophetic word, you are often unaware which phrases will endure and emerge as the most pivotal. It has taken me nine months to discover that the most resonant part of that prophetic vision and my interpretative words in March 2020 were these:

"…to many others this will be remembered as a time where you ask "What was all that about?!" – a time where fear and panic attempted to take over the hearts of men."

While many have indeed grieved this year, as the word stated, I do feel we are slowly entering a phase of this troubled season that will be marked as much by uprising and the questioning of the actions of governments and scientists, as by the pandemic itself.

What began early in 2020 as an apparent need for some kind of societal lockdown, while scientists established what kind of danger Coronavirus actually posed and hospitals handled a noticeable above-normal deathrate among many populations, eventually there also arose great disputes about data, exaggerated worst-case scenarios, unclear morbidity rates, hap-hazard advice and authoritarian legal constraints, imported globally from communist China's pandemic response.

While many have been content with the political response to the pandemic, others are rising up who have felt manipulated by fear-mongering methods from heavy handed politicians, ever-changing rules, the curtailing of basic liberties and blizzards of misinformation and disinformation from a hyperbolic press.

All this is leading, I believe, to a period where some will indeed grieve the sad loss of loved ones to a genuinely vicious virus, but others will rise up questioning the efficacy and justice of lockdowns, driving the poor into greater poverty, leaving cancer sufferers undiagnosed or untreated, mental health in crisis and countless businesses bankrupt. Some studies are already showing that the medium to long term excess deaths caused by lockdowns may be very significant indeed. (3a)

Globally, government actions trying to contain the pandemic were predicted to push 135 million people into severe hunger and starvation (1), while some studies showed up to 100 million adults and children could have been pushed into extreme poverty.(2) There could be as many as 1.1 million additional child deaths (3) and interrupted immunization programs put 80 million children at risk of contracting deadly diseases.(4) UNICEF expected 6,000 additional children under five could die a day. (5)

Japan's suicide rate rose 16% (6) while 48% of the UK's post-lockdown child suicide deaths related to Covid-19 or lockdown.(7) Also in the UK, thousands of children became at risk of abuse and exploitation in unregulated care homes,(8) 80% of young people said the pandemic made their mental health worse,(9) 1 in 6 children developed a probable mental disorder, (up from 1 in 9),(10) and many entire families, it was claimed, were being "swept into poverty" by the pandemic.(11)

Professor Philip Thomas of Bristol University estimated that the equivalent of 560,000 UK lives will be lost because of the "health impact of the deep and prolonged recession."(12)

In the UK a total of 30,260 excess deaths occurred in private homes in 2020, but less than 1 in 10 were due to COVID-19. (13) Online domestic abuse searches increased 352.5%,(14) depression and suicidal thoughts rose 26.1% (15) and loneliness and isolation were affecting 9 million in the UK.(16) 1 in 3 cancer patients' treatment was affected and 70% of them said their mental health suffered. Cancer screening was cancelled for 3 million,(17) 600,000 women missed their smear tests,(18) and excess deaths from heart disease rose 13%.(19) A third of the population increased their alcohol intake and 35% postponed seeking medical advice or treatment, a move many believe will lead to a rise in medium term deaths from undiagnosed terminal illnesses.(20)

The jobless rate in the UK rose to 6.5%,(21) retail sales in 2020 were the 'worst for 25 years' (22) and it was also the worst year for High Street job losses in the same period.(23)

This complex world period may well end with governmental leaders and advisors facing investigation and litigation, as the families of those who died as a direct result of government actions, rather than the virus itself, give way to waves of examination in the years that follow.

Peace In The Storm

And so I believe we are entering a period I would call *"What was that all about?!"* as an uprising of unrest seeks to clarify the events of the last months, and we slowly leave the most intense pandemic period behind, vaccines are distributed and society tries to find its way back to normal.

But in this time of uprising, how should the Christian respond?

Psalm 29 begins by assuring us of God's reign over a troubled earth. It shows us the power of God's voice to command and control, to speak and see events change. The Psalm concludes by encouraging us that *"The Lord gives strength to His people; the Lord blesses His people with peace."* (verse 11).

For the Christian this is a time for us to keep from both anxiety and denial, and simply to walk in peace and wisdom with our

God who reigns. It is time to care for our neighbours, to pray for the frail, to soothe the anxious and to comfort the grieving. It's a time to *"Speak out for those who have no voice"* (Proverbs 3:18) and advocate for the poor, to fill up foodbanks, to counsel those facing financial hardship, to pray for the sick and share the Gospel.

But it is not a time for us to be stirred up in fear like the world around us. It is a time rather to trust that God is indeed, *"enthroned over the flood"* to bring the evil to an end, and that we, His people, are the apple of His eye.

Indeed, it is little surprise to me, as anyone who has read my writings would know, that at this particular point in history some great, era birthing event would take place. This next chapter will show you exactly what I mean…

Sources

1a. See Notes in The Passion Translation for Psalm 29:10.
2a. https://jarrodcooper.net/2020/03/17/what-i-sense-god-is-saying-about-the-coronavirus/
3a. https://www.thelancet.com/journals/lancet/article/PIIS0140-6736(20)31422-7/fulltext

1. (BMJ/UN World Food Program) https://www.bmj.com/content/371/bmj.m4263
2. (UN website/World Bank/Unicef/Save The Children) https://www.un.org/development/desa/dpad/publication/un-desa-policy-brief-86-the-long-term-impact-of-covid-19-on-poverty/
3. (Lancet/Bill & Melinda Gates Foundation) https://www.thelancet.com/journals/langlo/article/PI-IS2214-109X(20)30229-1/fulltext
4. (New York Times/WHO/UNICEF/Vaccine Alliance) https://www.nytimes.com/2020/05/22/health/coronavirus-polio-measles-immunizations.html
5. (UNICEF) https://www.unicef.org/press-releases/covid-19-devastates-already-fragile-health-systems-over-6000-additional-children
6. https://www.theguardian.com/world/2021/jan/16/japans-suicide-rate-rises-16-in-second-wave-of-covid-study-finds
7. (National Child Mortality Database) https://www.ncmd.info/wp-content/uploads/2020/07/REF253-2020-NCMD-Summary-Report-on-Child-Suicide-July-2020.pdf
8. https://www.theguardian.com/society/2021/jan/06/thousands-of-children-sent-to-unregulated-care-homes-amid-covid.
9. (Young Minds) https://youngminds.org.uk/about-us/reports/coronavirus-impact-on-young-people-with-mental-health-needs/
10. (NHS) https://digital.nhs.uk/news-and-events/news/survey-conducted-in-july-2020-shows-one-in-six-children-having-a-probable-mental-disorder
11. https://www.theguardian.com/world/2021/jan/16/coalition-of-child-experts-urge-inquiry-into-uks-covid-crisis?CMP=Share_iOSApp_Other
12. https://www.spectator.co.uk/article/is-the-cost-of-another-lockdown-too-high-
13. (GP Online) https://www.gponline.com/gps-urge-government-consider-indirect-covid-19-harms-lockdown-decisions/article/1696300
14. https://www.england.nhs.uk/coronavirus/wp-content/uploads/sites/52/2020/05/C0376-domestic-abuse-duringpcovid-19-letter.pdf
15. (Samaritans) https://www.samaritans.org/news/new-study-reveals-mental-health-impact-initial-lockdown-period/?fbclid=IwAR0mNcWtUe0w7Rszu_Rc71FwG3nbyND-VS8CKBxMcvtVD-C6zOV2hqnGsls8
16. (Age UK/Mind). https://www.mirror.co.uk/news/uk-news/silent-epidemic-hit-nine-million-23291390
17. (Cancer Research UK) https://scienceblog.cancerresearchuk.org/2020/09/11/whats-happened-to-cancer-services-during-the-covid-19-pandemic/
18. (Caroline Nokes MP) https://www.dailymail.co.uk/news/article-9155363/Fears-600-000-women-risk-cervical-smear-tests-cancelled-missed-lockdown.html
19. (British Heart Foundation) https://www.bhf.org.uk/what-we-do/news-from-the-bhf/news-archive/2020/october/rise-in-excess-heart-and-circulatory-disease-deaths-in-under-65s
20. (Kings College London) https://www.kcl.ac.uk/news/nearly-a-third-of-uk-public-drinking-more-alcohol-than-usual-during-the-pandemic
21. (SKY News) https://news.sky.com/story/covid-19-boe-governor-about-2-2-million-unemployed-in-very-difficult-period-for-economy-12185707
22. (BBC) https://www.bbc.co.uk/news/business-55625246
23. (BBC) https://www.bbc.co.uk/news/business-55501049

JOURNAL TIME

Use the questions below to ponder and journal.

1. What areas of your life need a divine reset?

2. Has God been placing any areas of your life on pause lately? Why might this be?

3. What were your own experiences of the pandemic in 2020/21, and what has God been saying to you through this time?

4. Even in troubling times, God's people can know His peace. What things have been disturbing your peace lately, and how can you "cast your burdens on God" and enjoy His peace?

JOURNAL

1. My weight and my diet
What I watch and listen to
My energy levels

2. Fellowship with people of
the same spirit.
It will come in God's time

3. It was a completely different
experience. A lot less busy and
a time to reassess my life
It will be a new time but
more to come not what I
expected.

4. The deterioration in peoples
behaviour. Violence and
immorality. Focus on the promise
of God to give a clearer picture

JOURNAL

Chapter 2
A Pivot Point In History

"From one man he made all the nations, that they should inhabit the whole earth; and he marked out their appointed times in history and the boundaries of their lands."
- Acts 17:26

In July 2017 I sat outside The Queens House looking up towards the Royal Observatory in Greenwich, home of the Prime Meridian of the World, the site from where we get Greenwich Mean Time (GMT). It is the place where east meets west and where we on earth interpret solar time and align our clocks. In 1884 the Greenwich Meridian was recommended as the Prime Meridian of the World, the centre of world time and the basis for our global system of time zones.

You could say it is the place where the movement of the heavens are interpreted to give us timings on the earth.

And here I was, on a summer prayer and study sabbatical, looking out from an ancient royal home, toward the place where we look to the heavens to discern our times.

So of course, God spoke to me!

I had been living with a word from God for about 8 months – a word about the significance of the 2017, 500-year anniversary of the commencement of The Reformation – when Martin Luther sent lasting ripples of transformation through the world, simply by questioning the status quo.

In October 1517, 500 years ago, Luther had begun a powerful and surprising work of restoration in the Church, but that led me to ask if a 500-year era might have been significant in history before?

I know that God has often moved in specific seasons, Daniel 2:21 stating that God *"changes times and seasons; He deposes kings and raises up others"* and that He *"gives wisdom to the wise and knowledge to the discerning."* In Acts 17:26 the Bible says God *"determines our pre-appointed times."* I also know that in 1 Chronicles 12:32 it says that the sons of Issachar *"had understanding of the times to know what Israel ought to do."* God loves to reveal His seasons and timings to His people, so is there a secret for us to find in this time?

Seasons & Times

Numbers are incredibly important in the Bible. If you were to read my 2017 book "500" you would find a study of biblical numbers. The numbers 3, 7, 12, 40 are all significant and often define seasons, the completion of a cycle or mark some pivot point. But did you know the number 500 is important too? And most importantly, the number 500 might well deeply affect your life today, if you are alive anywhere near 2017! (1)

As I have studied Biblical and Church history, it would seem that approximately every 500 years some radical change takes place between God, how He interacts with mankind or how mankind grasps God's divine purpose.

By this I do not mean that everything changes at exactly 500 years to the minute, as the clock strikes midnight. I mean rather, that God moves like the slow turn of a giant battleship changing course in the ocean, about every 500 years or so. Every five centuries God's purposes on earth seem to haul us into a new age, slowly carving a new course on the seas of history, the change sometimes taking several decades to emerge. Like a heavy castle gate, swinging slowly on giant hinges, God takes mankind through a colossal historical adjustment that ultimately leads to the unfolding of His purpose for humanity.

Now pause as you read the next line because this is important:

You are alive at one of those turning points in history.

In "500" I take the reader back through eight, 500-year eras, so we can see that something extraordinary has taken place at the five century pivot point, every time:

It's 500 years from Noah and the flood, to Abraham and his family, and from Moses to David, from the Exile and great national turmoil, to Jesus Himself and the birth of the early Church.

Of course, Jesus is the most obvious of all great pivotal points in our history – when He came He split history between B.C. and A.D., between Old Testament and New, between Law and Grace and between the old flesh and the empowerment of the Spirit! Jesus, the cross and resurrection IS the greatest pivot point of all history.

But this pattern didn't stop with Jesus and the era of the Biblical writings. It is amazing that Jesus came just after the birth of the Roman empire in 31BC, allowing the Gospel to spread rapidly along those straight Roman roads for almost 500 years! In AD476 the Roman empire declined and we entered the 1000 year long Dark Ages.

500 years into the Dark Ages we find the Great Schism, where there was a break of communion between what are now the Eastern Orthodox and Roman Catholic churches due to in-fighting and the politicizing of power and authority across the Church. Then 500 years after that Great Schism, as the Dark Ages were ending, came the Reformation.

The 500-year pivot points are astonishingly clear.

The Reformation

On All Saints' Eve, 1517AD, after 1000 years of comparative Church powerlessness, a man called Martin Luther was about to become another pivotal character in global history. Luther publicly objected to the way preacher Johann Tetzel was selling indulgences (A supposed way to reduce the amount of punishment one has to undergo for sins) so he famously nailed his 95 Theses to a castle church door, calling for a public debate. His Theses spread across Germany causing shockwaves as he questioned the authority of the pope, a move which ultimately led to a transformation we can still feel today.

Luther was a man of faith who stood against the corrupt political power-game that the Church had become. He stood for the authority of scripture and the idea of salvation by grace. Little did he know that his actions would usher in 500 years of Reformation that would ultimately bring the Church back to her original passion, power and purpose.

Across the last 5 centuries, wave after wave of reforming and restoring power have washed the Church bringing her back to God's original design. To read more about all this, pick up my book "500" and discover the great pivot moments of history, including how the last 500 years have been an amazing era of reformation and restoration. You can also read the numerous prophetic words from across many decades, about what God is going to do next – the first waves of which are beginning to lap upon the shores of our own lives today.

Let me repeat the thought I want you to grasp from this chapter more than any other: *You are alive at a pivotal turning point in history.* It is no wonder to me therefore, that difficult global storm surges are announcing the change of eras, like the trumpets of heaven in the book of Revelation. You don't usually glide into new epochs; historically there is often more of a violent birthing that takes place!

New eras have been accompanied in the past by catastrophic events like global floods, invasions, exiles, conflicts, plagues, wars, occupations, genocide, infanticide, political exploitation, cruelty, murder and much grief.

Yet they are also marked as times of encounter, redemption, rescue, calling, glory, burning fire and blazing mountains, of God coming close and man being graced. They are usually great times of prophetic enlightenment, divine clarity, long-awaited fulfilment and surprising revelations, of healing, restoration, refreshing and renewal. They feel to the righteous as if the accumulation of years of longing, praying, seeking and prophesying, finally burst forth from the heavens and rain on the soil of our suffering, bringing to birth a new day.

You are alive in such a day.

So the great question now is, what comes next? What are the prophets saying now in response to this Divine Reset? This is not just the end of a 500-year era – we are at the BEGINNING of one! What will that era look like? What is going to happen? And what can we do to be ready for all God wants to do?

Read on. God has been speaking…

Sources
1 "500" by Jarrod Cooper - https://www.amazon.co.uk/500-Are-Dawn-New-Glory/dp/1908393742/ref=sr_1_2?dchild=1&keywords=jarrod+cooper&qid=1607431893&sr=8-2

JOURNAL TIME

Use the questions below to ponder and journal.

1. If God has *"marked out your appointed time in history"* (Acts 17:26) how can this bring you comfort and encouragement today?

2. You are important. You were born at one of the major 500-year pivot points in global history. How does this make you feel about your life?

3. If God desires to *"give wisdom to the wise and knowledge to the discerning"* how can you acquire greater wisdom from Him?

JOURNAL

The overall plan of my life is marked out by God. I may fail but He wont, never let me down. I have been waiting for this time in history to come and I know that it will be fruitful. I have faith and God will reward me. It is a time of encouragement and comfort for me.

That I am not or ever was overlooked or forgotten by God. My latter years will be greater than the former. and I draw great encouragement from that.

Ask as it says in James, biblical wisdom is not self-seeking it is for building up others and leading you through life.

JOURNAL

Chapter 3
The Shaking And The Storm

"Some things broke my heart but fixed my vision" – Anon

As excited as I am about the era before us, it would be remiss of me to simply jump to positive, exciting prophetic words and practical actions to get your life, ministry or church ready for what God is about to do next. I think we need to go a layer deeper first.

Can I confess something? I do have a tendency to be overly optimistic. My mind is a little more comfortable with heavenly bliss than the stormy mess of real life! So I'm going to rein in my desire to jump to the prophetic promises of heaven and instead pause and try to get a real spiritual world-view of what's happening in the earth right now. I think we all know it's a time of shaking, so let's take some moments to unpack the fact that this has been a stormy time for many of us, and why.

To start with, I know of no period in my lifetime, when the following passage has seemed more relevant globally, how about you?

"See to it that you do not refuse him who speaks. If they did not escape when they refused him who warned them on earth, how much less will we, if we turn away from him who warns us from heaven? At that time his voice shook the earth, but now he has promised, "Once more I will shake not only the earth but also the heavens." The words "once more" indicate the removing of what can be shaken—that is, created things—so that what cannot be shaken may remain. Therefore, since we are receiving a kingdom that cannot be shaken, let us be thankful, and so worship God acceptably with reverence and awe, for our "God is a consuming fire." Hebrews 12:25-29

In this most unusual of seasons I believe many of us are experiencing a turmoil, a shaking, major chaos and upheaval, but I think what is most confusing is that the shaking actually comes from many different sources. Several distinct things appear to be happening at once, some natural, some evil, some divine.

I can see at least five dynamic shakings at work right now. There is…

1) An agitation in the heavenlies (demonic realms/beings)

"Once more I will shake not only the earth but also the heavens" Hebrews 12:26 says. There is a heavenly realm of spiritual beings and authorities that is being stirred up at this pivot point in God's divine purposes. (See Ephesians 6:12)

2) A shaking, a groaning on the earth

Romans 8:20-22 says *"For the creation was subjected to frustration, not by its own choice, but by the will of the one who subjected it, in hope that the creation itself will be liberated from its bondage to decay and brought into the freedom and glory of the children of God. We know that the whole creation has been groaning as in the pains of childbirth right up to the present time."* The earth is being distressed by natural disasters, plagues and pain. The very earth itself is groaning, in the throes of a natural longing, awaiting the revelation of the sons of God.

3) The voice of God leading to the promise of a new era

"See to it that you do not refuse him who speaks" Hebrews 12:25 tells us at the start of this chapter's headline passage about a "shaking". As God speaks, it is more than mere information. He is unfolding, birthing, shaping the world. There is often an accompanying shaking.

In Psalm 29 we read:

"The voice of the LORD breaks the cedars;
*   the LORD breaks in pieces the cedars of Lebanon.*
He makes Lebanon leap like a calf,

Sirion like a young wild ox.
The voice of the LORD strikes
   with flashes of lightning.
The voice of the LORD shakes the desert;
   the LORD shakes the Desert of Kadesh.
The voice of the LORD twists the oaks
   and strips the forests bare."

When a being with God's limitless and unrivalled potency speaks, He may adjust Himself to bend down and whisper in your ear with a *still small voice*, but when God chooses to bellow His commands with a full-throated roar, universes are birthed, stars are flung into space and entire new dimensions are formed! No small wonder then that our little world *"leaps like a calf"* and our desert lands shake when He raises His voice!

In every shaking season, go in search of the voice of God. He's trying to get your attention! There is a voice in the shaking taking place globally right now, and we must give time to comprehend Him.

4) A judgement (correction) of God to the Church, as He lifts us to better ways ready for a new era

The fourth shaking at work right now is a judgment, or correction, taking place in the Church. Some Christians talk as if God no longer judges, punishes, chastises, or brings discipline. This merely reveals a lack of Biblical literacy and a probable over-emphasis on the doctrine of grace, without the appropriate tension towards judgement and holiness of conduct we find throughout the New Testament.

"For it is time for judgment to begin with God's household; and if it begins with us, what will the outcome be for those who do not obey the gospel of God?" 1 Peter 4:17

John 9:39 states *"Jesus said, 'For judgment I came into this world, that those who do not see may see, and those who see may become blind.'"*

John Piper writes in explanation of Jesus talk of judgement,

"This is at first jarring because Jesus said in two other places that he did not come to judge the world. In John 3:17, he says, "God did not send his Son into the world to judge the world, but in order that the world might be saved through him." And in John 12:47, he says, "I did not come to judge the world but to save the world."

But the contradiction is only apparent. It's not real. When Jesus says that he did not come to judge, he means that condemnation is not his first or his direct purpose. He is coming to save. When he says, "For judgment I came into the world," he means that inevitably, as I save people by truth and love and righteousness, a division happens and rebellion is revealed and people are confirmed in their unbelief." (1)

Of course, God's judgements are always seeking to redeem, restore, mature and improve our lives. He has "no plans to harm you" as the fridge magnet and prophet Jeremiah 29:11 states! So judgment for the Church is equivalent to the naughty step for your 4 year old – He is out to grow us up and line us up for blessing!

In a few chapters time we will investigate some of the key areas of judgment God is confronting the Church with in this day. I think you may find it enlightening.

5) The judgements of God in the world – justice issues & the unveiling of sin

Similarly, globally we can see God is shaking the world to unmask sin, collapse ungodly ideologies and even hand some over to the eventual consequences of evil behaviour. While God's grace is revealed in great patience with the Church and the world, eventually we all *"reap what we sow"* (Galatians 6:2) and passive or even direct judgement is often the result. The widespread unveiling and judgement of sin often comes with great societal upheaval, and you can see that is at work around the world right now, but more about that later in the book.

A Voice In The Shaking

Note in Hebrews 12 that while it speaks mainly of "shaking", its context is that *God is Speaking: "Do not refuse Him who speaks"* is the lead point in verse 25. The shaking then, often contains God's voice, even though grief or even evil may also be at work.

In all these terrible trials and turmoil, I most want you to see that God is speaking. Despite the turmoil He is speaking. Not everything that is happening is from God, but God will use everything. Even some of the justice issues He is bringing to the surface at this time may be muddled by man, confused or even swing towards revenge rather than justice – but we need to listen to God speaking through these events.

In the middle of this turbulent time, I have seldom known a more prophetic season. Visions, dreams and words from heaven seem to flow easily, every time I remove myself from the irritation and distraction of the world's shaking and give myself again to the stillness of His presence in the eye of the storm.

What To Do In A Shaking

It is not the first time God's people have found themselves in a season-change shaking. Some have even experienced lockdowns, but eventually found great deliverance, favour and renewed purpose has flowed, when they've discerned God's voice in the storm.

When Noah went through a storm season, he was saved, not by the Ark, but by His righteous walk with God (Genesis 6:9). The result was he went through the tumultuous season safely, into a bright new day of promise.

This is a time then to develop your intimate, personal walk with God. It will keep you calm when the world is in chaos, and carry you through to a new day. If you hide in the "Ark" of your walk with God, you're going to find He brings you out with favour and increase.

When the children of Israel went through the turmoil of the confrontation between Moses and Pharaoh, 10 plagues, and a period when things got worse, not better, at Passover they were to *"hide under the blood"* till the judgement had passed (Exodus 12:22). Then God led them into a powerful season of new glory, purpose and promise.

We too should hide under the blood of God's forgiveness and protection while this season passes by. If we stay close to Him, He will bring us out with plunder and blessing, ready to walk towards a new Promised Land.

When the disciples went through the turbulence and shaking of the death and resurrection of Jesus, they hid away in prayer, waiting for the promised power of the Holy Spirit in that upper room (Acts 1:14 & 2:1+). When the Spirit fell in fire, they were launched from lockdown into a season of promise and glory!

We too, must find our upper rooms of prayer, repentance, intimacy and devotion, that a fresh outpouring of power and presence would propel us into the new promised era as well.

This pivotal season of shaking has biblical and historical precedent. Let's dwell in the secret place of our walk with God, listening for His voice in the shaking. Let's hide under the blood of Jesus with repentant and soft hearts, willingly seeking deeper purity and maturity. Let's wait for the release of the Spirit empowering us into this new era in God, knowing that this could lead to His glory, harvest, revival, fulfilment and the Kingdom coming in the world!

Haggai Goes A Step Further

When the unknown author of Hebrews is writing of the shaking in chapter 12, he (or she) is quoting Haggai 2. Haggai's version is a tad longer, and with a significant conclusion as its finale:

*"This is what the LORD Almighty says: 'In a little while I will once more shake the heavens and the earth, the sea and the dry land. I will shake all nations, and what is desired by all nations will come, **and I will fill this house with glory,**' says the*

LORD Almighty." Haggai 2:6-7

Haggai reveals that the purpose of the shaking is that God's glory fills the temple - you could say the Church!

Haggai goes on:

'The glory of this present house will be greater than the glory of the former house,' says the LORD Almighty. 'And in this place I will grant peace,' declares the LORD Almighty." Haggai 2:8-9

Divine shaking, it would seem, has the capacity to lift us to new glories, where the weight of God's favour, blessing and power propels us further than ever before, the latter house becoming more glorified than the former.

If we could just co-operate with the great pause that we have found in the eye of this pandemic, what could take place? If we surrender to the Refiner's fire, if we are adjusted and upgraded to a place where we are ready for a fresh move of God, then I believe the result could be an outpouring of presence, power and glory that leads to a harvest of souls and the Kingdom Come in society. That is surely a worthy purpose for the shaking and storms we are living through?

Sources

1 https://www.desiringgod.org/messages/for-judgment-i-came-into-this-world

JOURNAL TIME

Use the questions below to ponder and journal.

1. I think the quote "Some things broke my heart but fixed my vision" is profound. Can you recall any time in your life where trial and even tragedy has also brought about some kind of good? What good things came of the difficulty?

2. What things are shaking right now globally and personally?

3. Can you identify specific shakings taking place in the 5 areas listed in this chapter? 1) In the heavenlies/spiritual. 2) In the earth/natural. 3) Because of God and His purposes. 4) Judgement in the Church. 5) Judgement in the world

4. What do you think God is saying to you through the current shakings and storms of life?

JOURNAL

1.

Romans 8:28

What satan meant for our God meant for good.
What came out of it was the beginning
of a new season that will bring
us into a new time. It is our time!

2. Economics, morality and Climate.

My thinking and actions are
not sufficient for this shaking!

3. Be strong, be patient "Trust in
Me. Keep your focus on what
Jesus and the Holy Spirit are
saying.

JOURNAL

Chapter 4
Positioned For Reset

"Opportunity does not waste time with those who are unprepared." - Idowu Koyenikan

Isaiah 43:18-19 is being cited by many as an apt scripture for this time:

"Forget the former things;
   do not dwell on the past.
See, I am doing a new thing!
   Now it springs up; do you not perceive it?
I am making a way in the wilderness
   and streams in the wasteland."

This well-thumbed verse in many a Bible is, of course, preached at many turning points in the lifetime of a church, family or team. It reminds us clearly that God still is both capable of, and wants to do, brand new things, things *"no eye has seen, no ear has heard, and no human mind has conceived"*. 1 Corinthians 2:9

Sometimes the greatest enemy of a new day, is our years of memory about how to do life and ministry. These can dull our hearts and minds to the point where we find ourselves repeating well-worn patterns from recollection, instead of striking out into new territories. Most of us who start out as pioneers, soon find ourselves settling, as the emotional and literal cost of new days and fresh ways takes its toll on our aging sense of adventure.

Even if we could muster up enough energy to crave new days, sometimes the strength of nostalgia, the sheer blinkering effect of powerful recollections and the capacity our minds have to live within our own narrative, means we can almost seem unable to even perceive what new things God might want. Most of us certainly look at change as less attractive as we age, and spend time gold-embossing nostalgic memories, that were never actually as idealistic as our minds tell us! It would seem that embracing new things requires an almost supernatural level of spiritual perspective.

This is difficult, because the verse in Isaiah makes it clear that to enter new times, requires the ability to perceive them. *"See, I am doing a new thing! Now it springs up; do you not perceive it?"*

It seems paramount that we somehow forget the past, and instead perceive and recognise God's new ideas when they arrive. It also informs us that it is far from automatic or intuitive to do so, otherwise it wouldn't need proclaiming by a prophet in the way Isaiah does!

But look again at the Ancient of Days: Isaiah teaches us that God is still pioneering pathways into deserts and uncharted territories, making previously uninhabitable places, habitable, with flowing streams bursting forth in arid lands.

Dreams we have given up on, He still has plans for. Ideas that simply would not support us, are no longer inhospitable deserts, but have streams of provision flowing like never before. Places where you could not bring up a family, will teem with life, and wastelands where the Gospel has failed to thrive in millennia, can suddenly embrace the Saviour with unbridled acceptance. There is a world of God's "new" beyond the limitations of our imaginations – if we could only see what He sees!

Entering the new is challenging. Entering a new *season* is hard enough, so how on earth do we enter a *whole new era*? Are there some mind-sets, postures and life-hacks that may help us step beyond our memories, into the world of God's imagination? I believe so.

Here are 8 attitudes I think optimise our ability to find a clear perception of God's new things:

1.   Be Well Travelled

By this, I don't even mean physical travel, but rather having a curious, wonder-filled soul. Experienced, culturally well-travelled leaders can spot the difference between what is eternal and temporal, cultural or divine, much quicker than those who are deeply entrenched in their own stream, denomination, national culture or history. Get out more, and you'll see more clearly. Read lots, podcast lots, visit lots (especially outside your normal stream) and you will be wiser.

2.   Be BIG Hearted

"Guard your heart, for out of it flow all the issues of life" Proverbs 4:23

Leadership and ministry is hard. It's easy to end up with a shrivelled, grumpy, cynical heart (Been there, done that!). Many leaders find themselves small-hearted as a result of protecting themselves from the "wars" of ministry life. But it also means you end up pessimistic, sarcastic, envious, distorted and jaundiced. Stay BIG hearted. You can tell if you are big-hearted by your innermost conversations about others, especially successful others. If you are envious, harsh, judgmental and protectionist, rather than kind, gracious and celebratory at the success of others – then you have some heart work to do, and your blinkered envious perspectives will hinder you perceiving what God is doing easily.

3.   Stay Organisationally Mobile

The best churches feel like movements, not clubs. This means changing scenery is part of the norm. "Dust settles" they say, and we are made of dust – our sinful flesh loves to settle and calcifies so easily. Make your church or team a place very used to the flexible world of fresh movement, by doing new things often (and even just for the sake of it!). Battle congregational brittleness, by making plasticity a cultural value. The result is that you will all embrace divine change more easily when it comes.

4.   Value Intimacy Above Method

Moses was kept out of the Promised Land by God, because he chose method over intimacy (Number 20:6-12). God considered it mistrust and therefore idolatry to "strike the stone" in pursuit of water, as he had been instructed in the past, instead of "speak to the stone" (the clear instruction God had given him this time).

Clinging to our methods, at the expense of listening to the still small voice of intimate instruction, is idolatry – and is far more common than we would like to admit. We all do it! Even the most informal Spirit-filled churches end up stuck in forms of their own liturgy! We need to spot it and get back to God's voice where necessary, as fresh worlds await us there.

The prophet Dr. Sharon Stone, who featured in the introduction of this book and is a dear friend, felt throughout 2019 that God was leading her into a year of trialling "A New Normal" – and what followed was a year devoid of all the usual patterns and predictability of ministry. It was now up to God to decide when they sang, preached, prophesied or had a social time, and many other things besides. It was a year of putting her L-Plates back on, listening more intently for God's voice and seeking to be more exact in obedience. The results were powerful!

At the start of 2020, when she was with us in Hull, God was saying to her *"We're going to do that again – The New Normal is here to stay!"* – Well, if that is not a prophetically accurate word for 2020 and beyond, I don't know what is! As we enter the "New Normal" of this new era, let's make a return to the intimate voice of God, and let Him have His Church back!

5.   Develop A Palate For The New

*"No one pours new wine into old wineskins. Otherwise, the new wine will burst the skins; the wine will run out and the wineskins will be ruined. No, new wine must be poured into new wineskins. **And no one after drinking old wine wants the new, for they say, 'The old is better.'"** Luke 5:37-39

When Jesus speaks of new wine needing new wineskins, He goes on to say that when we taste the new, we will say *"the old is better"* or as some versions put it *"the old wine is easier, more comfortable"* (Luke 5:39).

Wow… What an insightful analysis of human nature! Both new wine and new ways are sharp to the taste. New shoes pinch a little, unlike our old favourite pair. New-found healthy foods are less delicious, ask many a child! So we must train ourselves to develop a mature, adventurous palate, one that can cope with the harsher, uncomfortable taste of a new day, knowing that you will adjust, grow, and the payoff will be worth it!

There are certain things I love to do as I have done them for so long they feel second-nature; I am completely at home in their flow. They feel relaxing, easy, and I feel confident and at my best. I'll be honest, I much prefer to feel competent, confident and in control. I genuinely feel like a better person there. But recently I have felt challenged to set sail on some new seas, get my learning hat on and step out onto unfamiliar waters. I feel underconfident, unsure, a starter, an amateur and a learner. How about you?

Immature me wants to back off from activities that scare me, and return to well-trodden, comfortable territory. I'd happily deceive myself that these feelings of amateurish incompetence were signs of God's guidance to avoid the new! But adult me knows to tell my immature self that in order to embrace all God has for me, I need to remain a pioneering amateur. To remember the feelings I had when I first preached, led worship, stepped out. Trembling voices, deep uncertainty in my own skills and radical obedience are actually so attractive to God's great grace – so I tell myself *"C'mon Cooper, don't give up easily. Keep going until you start to enjoy the new!"*

And maybe you need to give yourself a good talking to as well. Join me on the new seas of obedient adventure, it could get very exciting!

6.   Develop New Alignments

"He who walks with the wise grows wise, but a friend of fools suffers harm." Proverbs 13:20

Those you hang around affect you more deeply than you realise. We absorb attitudes, gifts, perspectives, and strengths (and weaknesses – be warned!). I have been blessed to be around some remarkable apostles and prophets of late, and I have felt myself physiologically and spiritually changed, just by being near them (Oh yes, your brain biologically changes when you experience new things).

Make some new friends, ones who are ahead of you spiritually, in influence or intellectually and you will be broad enough to enter a new season. This is a time of new alignments, and they are vital, not optional, in this new era.

7.   Rest Is A Weapon

As soon as we entered lockdown, church leaders had to begin thinking about changing almost everything, as multiple departments closed, public settings shut down and most endured the huge discovery curve of taking many ministries, groups and services online. Adrenaline pumped and it was actually a tad exciting (apart from those touched by grief or real anxiety in the moment).

But months into the pandemic the adrenaline had subsided and, for some, fatigue or even exhaustion, has visited your life. That is normal and even to be expected. But it also has certain dangers that we must avoid.

You see, fatigued me just wants life to go back to normal! Fatigued me is so tired of making decisions with so few proven reference points. Everything is new! It's draining. Fatigue will cause you to be irritated at your team, rush decisions, dictate decisions just to get things over with, or even freeze and procrastinate, unable to make a decision at all. Oh, I've been there, with or without a pandemic!

But refreshed you will be able to flex with the new season. Your mind will be willing to percolate new information, your emotions will be energised enough to care for your team, your body will get you out of bed, ready to face another day of new opportunities. For most of us, when we are rested we are optimists, when we're exhausted, we're pessimists. You need to give your church and team a rested you.

This year I have discovered a weekly sabbath like never before. For me it's day to switch off the phone, do no work or DIY, and cease from even the thought of work or ministry. A day purely for gratefulness, family, resting in God, making room for joyful pleasures and having fun together.

It's not meant to be a day of cranky religious observance, but instead a day gifted to you since creation as a holy time of replenishment, restoration, reflection and refreshing. The very first thing God made holy in the Bible was a 24-hour period every seven days, as a gift of respite to you, and even science has shown, you are wired in sinew and soul to function best when you embrace it.

"By the seventh day God had finished the work he had been doing; so on the seventh day he rested from all his work. Then God blessed the seventh day and made it holy, because on it he rested from all the work of creating that he had done." Genesis 2:2-3

Resting for a weekly Sabbath is one of the 10 commandments, and while some would say we are no longer under Law, I would reply *"Which of the other 9 are you happy to break then? Murder, adultery, stealing, lying perhaps?"* You wouldn't dream of breaking the other 9 commandments, so why this one? We might consider rest as optional, but God considers it a "Top 10 Priority"! It is of course lazy theology to simply discard the Sabbath as a mere throw-back from the Old Testament, as if it were some obscure Pharisaical detail.

While I don't think it has to be a Saturday, or even Sunday, you do need to rest weekly, or else it may be a sign that something idolatrous is at work in your life. A striving to achieve, a consumerist hankering for more, a longing for approval, or even a fear of missing out. Some dread the very sound of their own souls and use busyness to mask the unhappiness within. But the godly know how to embrace silence, solitude and the joy of Sabbath.

Jesus put it this way:

"The Sabbath was made for man, not man for Sabbath" Mark 2:27

John Mark Comer pens it beautifully in his outstanding book "Garden City: Work, Rest and the Art of Being Human":

"That's why Sabbath is an expression of faith. Faith that there is a Creator and he's good. We are his creation. This is his world. We live under his roof, drink his water, eat his food, breathe his oxygen. So on the Sabbath, we don't just take a day off from work; we take a day off from toil. We give him all our fear and anxiety and stress and worry. We let go. We stop ruling and subduing, and we just be. We "remember" our place in the universe. So that we never forget . . . There is a God, and I'm not him."

God is offering you the incredible gift of trusting Him so completely that you can cease from work completely for a whole day a week. It is a weapon. It is a sign of inner health. It is not a second class use of your time. And it also seems to be one of the major prophetic words to Church leaders globally in this season. So don't ignore it. Make sure you're rested. A rested leader is a better leader whose mind will be refreshed enough to perceive a new day.

8.   Seek His Face

As leaders we must never lose the ability to "clear the decks" and strike out a morning, day, week, month or a long sabbatical to seek God and hear Him afresh. We cannot live on fast spiritual food, snatched between busy work – we must eat at Fathers banqueting table. To give time to pray, listen, study, worship, read, visit or simply sit in His presence. We cannot grow fresh ways of thinking from tiny margins of input. Deep change takes time.

As entire churches we must also be able to slow our work down and give time to seek God again. To allow some fields to lay fallow. To be able to cease, stop and even end projects entirely is a sign of church wellbeing. It teaches our churches not to run headlong at life, but to pause, to Sabbath, 'Selah', reflect, and listen to what the Father is saying. Church is not a mere human endeavour, but a divine idea – so we must let the Architect speak!

I have given days, weeks and even months to periodically seek God throughout my ministry, and each time I have come away with a fresh energy, plan and blueprint from heaven. How can we bring heaven to earth, if we will not take the time to be in the Strategy Rooms of the King? Plan the time, or else God might simply exile you to Patmos, to enforce you to rest in His presence! Ha! (Revelation 1:9-10)

"He who began a good work in you will carry it on to completion, unto the Day of Christ." Philippians 1:6

As you attempt to posture your life, family, team or entire church to be ready to embrace something radically new from heaven, remember the power of grace to lift you, change you and help you turn a corner. God is willing you to succeed more than you want to! He is committed to carry your destiny to completion.

Remember the power of the Spirit to make something more of you than you are. Remember His kindness will never let you down – so while you may not feel the most agile leader around, if you are genuinely crying out to God for wisdom, and are willing to humbly go where He says, I know you will find Him leading you.

JOURNAL TIME

Use the questions below to ponder and journal.

1. How good at perceiving new things are you?

2. Which of the 8 things that help clear perception are you best at?

3. Which of the 8 things that help clear perception do you need to develop the most?

JOURNAL

1 Moderate to good, I perceive
thing regularly

JOURNAL

Chapter 5
Turning It Off And On Again

"It is not the answer that enlightens, but the question."
– Eugene Ionesco

Early in 2020's first full lockdown, when all our in-person Revive Church work lessened greatly and the only ministry that could continue was online services, plus a few focussed outreaches through lunch clubs for those suffering food poverty, foodbank ministries, debt counselling and detached youth work on the streets, it left me personally with great periods of time to stop and reflect. To think deeply. To ponder with God on the first 50 years of my life, the direction of our church, my family, pretty much *everything*. It was a time to analyse the work, the remaining hopes and the dreams, to read old prophetic words and seek God for some fresh ones.

When Psalm 46:10 states *"Be still and know that I am God"* it literally means to stop, to cease, to "down tools" and halt working. To "sabbath" you could say. I know from my experience 3 years earlier when I was graced to enjoy a 2 month "sabbatical" that it brought great enlightenment and fresh energy. "Ceasing" for a period is one of God's greatest weapons against the driving religious spirit that grips many leaders like me! Learning to cease is a divine quality with many benefits.

If you've ever watched the T.V. show "The I.T. Crowd", with its farcical take on the technical department of a large fictitious organisation, you'll remember with a smile no doubt, that most problems were solved with the simple adage *"Have you tried switching it off and on again?"* – An amusing mantra that is closer to the realities of many an I.T. department than we'd like to admit!

But I think we resonate with the amusing and simplistic solution because there really is a great truth about switching things off and on again! And not just for computers, tablets, phones or other electronic devices – Resetting; stopping, ceasing, pausing, waiting, then slowly powering up again, is something even God uses with the world, and not least, His people. From a weekly Sabbath, to our need to pause and sleep well each night, God has built reset into the world.

In grander, but less frequent ways, God has also used reset to launch new global developments. When God brought judgment upon the world in Noah's day, was that flood not a global reset? A restart. A "take things back to basics and start again" period? A pruning back to a mere stump, and allowing things to grow back healthier, while retaining all the goodness in the root?

And when God removes a king and replaces him with a new leader, when He leads a prospective prophet into the wilderness, or when He forces us to "pause by still waters" (Psalm 23) ready for the next chapter of our lives, is He not performing a reset? When He causes His disciples to hide in an upper room, awaiting whatever will come next, or even when He allows invasion, scattering or regime change, all of which take place again and again in the Bible – are these not God taking His people through a divine reset?

The joy to be found in these times is that His ultimate aim is to turn His purposes powerfully "Back on again" as we enter a brand new chapter, with a line drawn in the sand that leaves any failure and mission drift behind us, that we may embrace the fresh pathways of His purposes with new vigour.

And this time has been such a reset time for me. In my season of pausing, He has led me kindly through countless deep, soul-searching and heaven seeking questions, some nudging my soul towards a better perspective, while some have carved great lumps out of my ego! He has, I believe, been leading me through a divine reset, and throughout this time the questions have been tough and direct, though laced with the smile of His grace.

Some of the dozens of questions God has placed before me over the last season I have compiled into five key areas for you. Perhaps these questions will help you shift towards the new era God has for you too?

1.   My Posture

Is my approach to life healthy? Are my heart, mind, body and soul in a ready posture to enter the new era? Am I supple, surrendered, fully in love with Him? Am I being faithful in the small, practical things? (Don't be discouraged, many will answer "No" – so ask a further question: *"What can I do to improve the posture of my life?"*)

2.   My Purpose

Can I clearly see God's purpose for me in the new era? What does God want to do with the rest of my life? Why was I born? Am I accurately fulfilling God's purpose for me, or have I drifted or even run, from them? (You might want to list some unfulfilled prophetic words/dreams given you or ask, "What am I passionate about or gifted in?" Best of all, take time listening to God.)

3.   My People

What close relationships do I need for entering the new era? Is my marriage healthy? Am I in the right spiritual relationships for the next phase of my life? Are there any connections that are bad for me, and that I need to put at a little more distance, or even cut off all together? Am I in the right church family, and I am going deep enough there?

4.   My Purity

Am I doing, thinking, saying or avoiding anything that I need to change, to line up with God's will for my life? Am I compromising in any small ways, and making excuses for sin? Am I still trusting God's grace to change my behaviours and my beliefs? List the areas where you feel convicted to change, ask for God's forgiveness and receive it fully (forgive yourself too!). Then write a list of the changes, with practical plans if necessary, to help bring new development in these areas. Ask God for grace to help you.

5. His Power

Am I still trusting God for miracles? Am I living a supernatural life, or have a dumbed down this supernatural adventure to the point where I need no Divine intervention anymore? What mountains of difficulty do I need God's divine power to move in this next era? How should I change my daily trust and declaration to see them move? Start to pray daily over your impossibilities, asking God to move on your behalf.

Resetting Our Responsibilities

To add to the personal reflections above, which have sliced deeply into my soul in this season, I also began to feel a strong sense that I needed to pick up more responsibility for my personal calling in a new way. We must regularly make sure we are seeing our lives from God's divine perspective - You and I were made to rule, to carry responsibility. We must never abdicate the throne God gives us, simply by looking at life from the place of a victim or with mere earthly perspective.

"Then God said, "Let us make mankind in our image, in our likeness, so that they may rule over the fish in the sea and the birds in the sky, over the livestock and all the wild animals, and over all the creatures that move along the ground."

So God created mankind in his own image,
in the image of God he created them;
male and female he created them.

God blessed them and said to them, "Be fruitful and increase in number; fill the earth and subdue it. Rule over the fish in the sea and the birds in the sky and over every living creature that moves on the ground." Genesis 1:26-28

God's mandate for mankind is that we should rule wherever we are. The New Testament only strengthens this theme:

"For if, by the trespass of the one man, death reigned through that one man, how much more will those who receive God's abundant provision of grace and of the gift of righteousness reign in life through the one man, Jesus Christ!" Romans 5:17

Of course, we must consider ruling and reigning with divine eyes, and not through the fallen lenses of fleshly or cruel authority. To rule with godliness is to take responsibility, to nurture, to protect, to guide and to serve. To discipline where required, but also to love deeply.

There is no room here for authoritarian heavy handedness or being a control freak. Rather we are to subdue the world with kindness, to fill the earth with grace, to be as clear a picture of our loving Heavenly Father as we can. That is leadership as our Father models it.

Here are five more questions to ponder about your own calling, the responsibility God has given you on the earth, and whether you are approaching that call from a place of weariness and fear, or faith, joy and divine hope:

1. You were made to rule in life by God's grace, over a) yourself b) a sphere of influence at home c) for most, some additional spheres of responsibility (e.g. work, justice, societal and/or within the Church). Can you list the spheres of influence you are, could be or should be influencing?

2. If money was no object, and your fears did not exist, what spheres of influence would you dream of being responsible in? (e.g. family, business, youth, evangelism?)

3. Are there any inner thoughts or perspectives, about yourself, God or others, that are making you avoid ruling with responsibility in these areas?

4. Many don't realise it, but when you die, you won't end up sitting on a cloud, playing a harp forever! You will in fact work and carry responsibility forever in the next life on "the new earth" (Oh, this is a whole other book to be written, right?!) If this life is training for the next, how could your respon-

sibility today, line you up for a powerful eternal life, then?

5. In the Bible we find that a) Intimacy with God, b) Your iden-
    tity, c) Your destiny and d) Your responsibilities, are una-
    voidably linked. You cannot do without any of these four,
    or else you end up in some deception or error. Intimacy
    is that love of being close to God. Identity is correctly un-
    derstanding who He has made you to be. Your destiny is
    knowing what He has called you to do and being faithful
    with your responsibilities is where you joyfully accept the
    obligations and pressures of that call. Most of us are usually
    weaker, or negligent, in one or more of the four areas. We
    may love intimacy but shun responsibility and thus never
    obediently live out God's purpose for our lives. This actually
    renders our intimacy as empty! (Luke 6:46) Alternatively, we
    may love to be busy about Church work, but have no clear
    understanding of who God has called us to be, or we may
    avoid intimate time with God altogether (Mark 7:7). Identify
    which of the four is your weakest area, and that may inform
    you where you need to invest next. Is it intimacy, identity,
    destiny or carrying the weight of responsibility?

Resetting The Church

This period of reflection has not only been good for me as a
person, but also for us as a church. It is so easy in the hustle and
bustle of church life to experience mission drift, and to slowly,
subtly, veer off course over the years. This results in us wasting our corporate energies in fruitless endeavours, things that
aren't relevant anymore, but we continue as it's complex to end
them! We spend vast amounts of our budget on things that
aren't productive, or live with perspectives regarding our purposes, our people and our priorities that are actually decades
out of date, as we haven't properly analysed them for years.

"Don't be too self-reflective" one leader gruffly wrote to me,
when speaking about the need to pause, reflect and think. *"We
need to stay proactive, there's a world to win!"*

But I don't find that stance biblical at all. What use is it being proactive at something that isn't working – If something is

not saving souls, transforming the world or discipling nations it needs careful consideration – and that doesn't always come easily in the rush of the busy week!

Our Master Jesus spent a little over 10% of His life in public ministry (that we know of). Just 3 ½ years out of His 33 were actually spent *"busy about his Fathers business"* (Luke 2:49), which would tell me God actually needs very little time to do remarkable things! Accuracy outperforms busyness. And accurate wisdom requires godly reflection.

If Jesus was willing to wait 30 years before ministering, and even then He started with 40 days alone in the wilderness to be fully ready for His purpose, then I'm going to give myself to reflection, sabbath, pondering and prayerful seasons.

During this pit-stop pause, at Revive Church we have reflected greatly on all our ministries, our leadership, our structures, our budgets, our purposes and their supporting goals, strategies and personnel.

Our conclusion was that we were out of shape! Mission-drift had led to deep weariness, higher spending and lower fruit than we would want. Certain aspects of our strategy were due a good prune. With some things, the concept of *"digging around the tree"* (Luke 13:8) and giving a project another season to find fruitfulness had been attempted several times. We now had to dismantle, disassemble and deconstruct some things in order to reinvent, reinvigorate and reset, ready for the new era ahead.

Here are some of the far-reaching questions we have been asking ourselves as a church leadership, to help lead us towards a vision and structure fit for the new era:

1. Is our structure life-giving, or smothering? Does it truly support, or just slow us down?
2. Is our current plan and strategy delivering the results we hoped for?
3. If we were starting Revive Church again, with our current members and income, what would we do differently?

4. Are our priorities truly biblical, or have we experienced mission drift? Are we too dependent on copying what other great churches are doing?
5. Are we being true to our unique calling as a church family? What are the prophetic words, the evident grace gifts in our leadership and what are the opportunities we feel passionate about, if we only had the time, focus and income?
6. What isn't working? Why haven't we stopped these things? Is it time to try again, to reshape, redefine or prune away these things?
7. Where are the signs of God's favour and fruit most evident?
8. Are our external denominational, apostolic, prophetic and internal leadership relationships up to date and relevant to where we are at today, or are we trapped in historical relationships that no longer bring life to our purpose today? Are there some relationships we need to move on from, or they move on from us?
9. Are we good at ending things like relationships, projects, goals, ministries, or do we only know how to add new things? Are we bold and loving with tough conversations or are we passive aggressive and cowardly? Have we learnt to end things without need for great conflict, blame or relational pain? Is our culture of honour mature enough to end things with dignity, love and celebration?
10. Do we feel like we are on an adventure, as a "band of brothers (and sisters!)" taking the world for Jesus, or have we become boring, middle class, mediocre and safe?
11. Are we building an empire for our own ego or are we truly building God's "Kingdom", where every church is part of one team, God's Team! Does our language, planning, metrics and budget reflect this?
12. Are we innovating, or simply repeating ministry patterns from memory?
13. How could we reach and transform our entire region for Jesus quickly? If Jesus was returning in 3 months, what would we do to reach people in that time?
14. What are our limitations and weaknesses, and how are we fixing or working around them?
15. Are we doing all we can to raise up the young, or are we simply content to grow old and safe together?
16. Are we valuing the older, wiser fathers and mothers among

us and harnessing their great wisdom, experience and stability?

17. Are we growing by reaching new Christians, or are we too happy to grow by picking up people floating in from other churches?

18. Are all the elements of the early church in the book of Acts allowed to thrive among us, or have we become a comfortable, westernised, consumerist church, simply happy to have bums on seats, but not passionate about the Kingdom coming among us?

19. Is our entire concept of Church fully biblical? Is it truly what Jesus imagined when He said *"Go into all the world"* or have we drifted into becoming a club for Christians?

20. Is it time for the senior leader to change? Are we ready for succession? Are we creating an environment where succession will be natural and healthy?

What a list?! Well, if you are half as challenged as I am in writing it, then you've got work to do in reflecting, pondering, discussing, adjusting and calling on God's grace to help you!

I have always said that *"frustration is usually the first prophet in any new move of God"* – Frustration calls out in our hearts like a signal from heaven. We may feel exasperated, disappointed, bored, rebellious or just plain thirsty for God. But these longings lead somewhere. It's God speaking. Don't push it away.

All great moves of God begin with frustration, but frustration drives us into prayer and into the wilderness of transformation, ready to reset in preparation for a new era with God.

JOURNAL & SESSION 1 DISCUSSION TIME

Use the questions below to ponder and journal, or to discuss this chapter with your small group or team.

This chapter is packed full of questions, spread across three sections. Rather than repeat all the questions here, I will refer you back to the passages for reflection and discussion.

1. Why is it important to reflect and *"give thought to your ways"* (Proverbs 4:26)?

2. Spend time pondering the 5 questions about your own **posture, purpose, people, purity** and need for God's **power**, that are early in this chapter. Write out or discuss where you need to improve, where you are doing well, and prayerfully ask God to help you.

3. Take time to consider the "**Resetting our Responsibilities**" section in the middle of this chapter. Consider the 5 questions carefully, both personally and as a group/team, to discover whether you are ruling as you should, or abdicating in some area.

4. Finally, dive into the 20 questions under "**Resetting The Church**" alone or as a team. Yes, this entire chapter may well take longer than one session, but fear not, we will return to many of the themes later in the book!

JOURNAL

JOURNAL

PART 2

THE WORD OF THE LORD

Chapter 6
What Is God Saying?

"There are few things more powerful than a life lived with passionate clarity." - Erwin McManus

At the start of this new decade, before we'd even heard of the Coronavirus or begun to imagine the concept of a reset, pause or pitstop, God gave me Isaiah 60 to share with our church. It reads:

"Arise, shine, for your light has come,
*   and the glory of the Lord rises upon you.*
See, darkness covers the earth
*   and thick darkness is over the peoples,*
but the Lord rises upon you
*   and his glory appears over you.*
Nations will come to your light,
*   and kings to the brightness of your dawn.*
"Lift up your eyes and look about you:
*   All assemble and come to you;*
your sons come from afar,
*   and your daughters are carried on the hip.*
Then you will look and be radiant,
*   your heart will throb and swell with joy;*
the wealth on the seas will be brought to you,
*   to you the riches of the nations will come.*
Herds of camels will cover your land,
*   young camels of Midian and Ephah.*
And all from Sheba will come,
*   bearing gold and incense*
*   and proclaiming the praise of the Lord.*
All Kedar's flocks will be gathered to you,
*   the rams of Nebaioth will serve you;*
they will be accepted as offerings on my altar,
*   and I will adorn my glorious temple."*

Being my usually overly positive self, I tend to concentrate on the spine-tingling verses that speak of the glory of God, the arrival of His divine Light, the gold, the gatherings and the glorious temples. But, as the troubling chaos of 2020 began to unfold, verse two seemed to resonate much more strongly:

"See, darkness covers the earth
  and thick darkness is over the peoples."

It is easy to forget that the context for glory is often darkness. The Bible is full of the twin train-tracks of pain and promise, failure and favour, trouble and triumph. God turns up in man's darkest days with His wonderful glory again and again throughout the pages of scripture.

Noah finds favour and a new beginning through a flood of terror and judgement. In the dangerous dust-bowl of the desert, God's people see His fiery glory on a mountain and over a holy Tabernacle. While grieving the loss of a good king, Isaiah encounters God's glory shaking the temple and cleansing him for service. At the command of a foreign emperor Jesus' heavily pregnant, socially ostracised mother, travels 90 miles on foot (or a little donkey perhaps?) to give birth in the stable of a near eastern house, nestled in the little subjugated town of Bethlehem. Yet this stressful and traumatic season in her life was punctuated with heavenly glory, angelic visitations and worshipping Magi. Even with Jesus' own arrival, God's glory brought a comfort in the days of trouble and tragedy.

And why would it be any different today?

God's Word For The New Era

As we have approached this pivot point in history, God has been unfolding His word layer after layer. Below I want to summarize the main points of His prophetic words to me and many prophets across the world, and in the next few chapters I will deepen and expand on the themes, adding various new perspectives and helping us to formulate our responses as individuals and teams.

I believe this Divine Reset, this Great Pause and Pit-Stop, is all aimed at preparing us for the following developments as the Church of the Living God.

As we enter this new era I believe that God is saying…

…Out of the storms and shaking of this new dawn will form in my people a clear new vision, accompanied by an unveiling of fresh power, purity and my strategies for this time.

In the midst of the shaking, a movement of my judgement and justice has been sweeping the earth and will not cease until I have accomplished all that needs to be prepared for this new time. A cleansing of my people is at work in your hearts and a breaking out from injustice is at work in the world. There is yet more to be unveiled, more to be confronted, more to be purified and cleansed, ready for the next great movement of my Spirit in the earth, but do not fret, I am at work in the midst of the fear, storms and limitation.

I am calling my people back to the Prayer Rooms in droves in this season, to encounter my presence and thus release my glory among you. My jealousy for your intimacy is calling out to your heart! And from that undistracted place will flow waves of outpouring, releasing miraculous power and the amplification of my voice in your heart. Dreams, visions, encounters, visitations and manifestations will become increasingly common place for you, as I gradually raise the intensity of my presence among you. You are to be found in my Strategy Rooms receiving fresh blueprints for this season, forsaking old methods, and embracing new grace and mantles prepared long ago for you.

From the Prayer Rooms and the Strategy Rooms will rise in you an embracing of the Kingdom mandate to "restore all things" (Acts 3:21) like no generation has ever done before. Your hearts will break over the state of your nation, city, neighbours and work colleagues. This is about more than just a harvest, though many souls will be saved. This is about restoration and Kingdom Come. The passion for transformation will begin to stir in you like "a fire shut up in your bones" (Jeremiah 20:9). You will no longer be content to "play church" and waste time on the mere trinkets of Christianity. I am releasing in you a sense of responsibility for your land and for your world because it is time for the re-ordering of all things, until one day you will say "the kingdoms of this world have become the kingdoms of our God" (Revelation 11:15).

This stirring that is growing in your heart, even now, will lead to a journey of personal reinvention and divine innovation, resulting in a transformation of the very behaviours, methods and even the beliefs of many Christians. While the essentials of my Gospel remain untouched, rather than live safely within the doctrinal walls of your favoured denomination, I am calling you out to a brave new era through the unveiling of new ideas, new graces and new perspectives in ministry. Some will call it a new Age of Innovation in the Church. Adventure, explore, run in the sheer joy of my counsel my people, for I am about to perform a wonder in the earth that will usher many into the Kingdom!

The prideful pretence of unity among my people grieves my heart, and so I am about to release a fresh grace in you for new collaborative endeavours. You will be over-joyed with the work of grace in your heart that begins to find pure, selfless pleasure in the family of my people. Rather than conducting mere unity events, I will empower you to walk in a new spirit of collaboration, partnership and alliance. I am also forming great new apostolic tribes of brothers and sisters in this day, all joined in love, filled with joy, kissed with my favour. Many of the old organisational structures of your youth will be deconstructed and crumble at the weight and speed of the innovations, pace and glory about to be released. Look for true fellowship, for there you will find my favour.

I am releasing the "spirit of Elijah" upon the earth once again (Matthew 17:11-13). The hearts of the fathers and the children will be brought to a place of sweet unity (Malachi 4:5-6). I am no longer content to move only in the middle ground - I am moving to the edges and releasing a glory over the little children and an empowering upon an older generation. This will be a sign in the earth: "Little ones will lead them" (Isaiah 11:6) while your "old men will dream dreams" (Acts 2:17) and their hearts will "throb and swell with joy!" (Isaiah 60:5). Look out for the rise of the Fathers and Mothers in the Church like never before. A new mission mandate is being placed before the older generation, who will embrace the call to mission even in their final years on earth – a generation is arising that will seek me for "refirement more than retirement!"

With every new movement of heaven there is a sound, and this day shall be no different. From the Prayer Rooms of my House I hear a new sound arising. It is a sound of war, a sound of worship, a sound of declaration and victory – but you shall not only hear the sounds of my people as they are stirred, but also the sounds of heaven. The trumpet blasts of my purposes are being released, the mobilised angelic hosts are cheering, the joy of the whole earth is come among you! You cannot be silent my people, you must sing, you must shout, you must declare – let us do that together, you and I, heaven and earth in unison! Many worship ministries will be lifted from the human platforms of the earth, to the throne room of heaven in this coming era. Many will sing as if seeing the very face of God. Prophetic psalmists will melt the hearts of the authorities of this earth, and as I did in Jehoshaphat's day, my glory will be revealed among the praises of my people. Let your new sound arise!

So my people, do not be afraid. Faint not. This is not an end, but a beginning. And what is more, I Am with you, I have gone before you. You shall not fail, but rather all will be unveiled, and we shall stride the earth together in this time, that the Kingdom would be seen in the nations.

AMEN! Let it be Lord!

For the remainder of our time together we're going to unpack and deepen these prophetic statements, preparing our hearts and minds for God's new purposes. We will seek to pivot our teams and churches ready for the new normal God is bringing to us and ready our lives for action.

JOURNAL & SESSION 2 DISCUSSION TIME

Use the questions below to ponder and journal, or to discuss this chapter with your small group or team.

1. Why might dark and difficult times, go hand in hand with glorious times in God?

2. Which phrases of the prophetic word in this chapter resonated with you most?

3. 1 Thessalonians 5:20 says *"Do not despise prophecies"* and the next verse says, *"test everything; hold fast what is good."* How can you "test" the prophetic word outlined in this chapter?

4. Do you have any personal or corporate unfulfilled prophetic words of your own? Recount and discuss them.

5. How could you improve the release of prophecy, the testing of prophecy and the collation and use of prophecy in your life/team/church? What good impact might such improvements have on your life/culture?

JOURNAL

JOURNAL

JUDGEMENT AND JUSTICE

7

The Lord says...

"In the midst of the shaking, a movement of my judgement and justice has been sweeping the earth and will not cease until I have accomplished all that needs to be prepared for this new time. A cleansing of my people is at work in your hearts and a breaking out from injustice is at work in the world. There is yet more to be unveiled, more to be confronted, more to be purified and cleansed, ready for the next great movement of my Spirit in the earth, but do not fret, I am at work in the midst of the fear, storms and limitation."

Chapter 7
Judgement & Justice

"Judgement begins with the House of God" 1 Peter 4:17

While much of the world's headlines have been taken up with talk of pandemics, lockdowns and vaccines of late, you would be forgiven for thinking that we would have little time for other controversial issues to grab our attention.

And yet the world is awash with much more than the pandemic. I found it amazing that at the height of the first lockdown in the U.K.'s spring of 2020, there was a brewing cauldron of racial unrest boiling up on the streets of the United States.

"I Can't Breathe"

The death of George Floyd at the hands of the U.S. Police force led to widespread protests, some of it violent and some peaceful, all gathered under the banner of George's now globally renowned final words *"I can't breathe"* – the phrase he gasped out while suffocating under the merciless grinding knee of a police officer.

This U.S. event led to global protests in many cities. At a time when half the planet was encouraged to socially distance themselves, multiple thousands teemed in our streets, objecting to a danger more damaging to them than any novel virus: *Racism and bigotry.*

Now while the actual objectives of the organisation labelled "Black Lives Matter" do leave much to be desired for any true Christian who researches them (They seem to be about much more than racism), that doesn't mean God isn't speaking, revealing, unveiling and unmasking an injustice that is not quite as resolved as many white people would like to think today.

Putting aside B.L.M.'s wider political intentions, the injustice of racism, the sin of bigotry and bias, and the hatred of one man for another, is an area of enduring sin God is unveiling right now, even in His Church. And not only is racism firmly on God's agenda, issues like abortion, cruel dictatorships, unhealthy political alliances, the plight of Israel and the Middle-East, the continuing growth of sex trafficking, the predicament of orphans, refugees and the poor are all resolutely part of God's Divine Reset in the earth today.

Though the ungodly may interpret this judgement and justice period as a time of revenge and violence, something no Christian should endorse, we must not be defensive and throw the baby out with the bathwater. We must remain soft-hearted, tender and sensitive enough to grasp that God is calling "Time" globally on many things, from predatory film makers, to bigoted employers, from perverse and abusive clergy, to the twisted abortion industry, from fraudulent election officials to power mad politicians.

Peering through the tempest of our world's headlines, awash with broadcasting hype and hyperbole, lies, exaggerations and the worst of all sins, the "half-truth", as Christians we should be able to make out our God in the midst of the squall, judging, revealing, bringing down leaders, unveiling sin, proclaiming "Enough is enough" on oppression, perversion, abuse, cruelty and bigotry.

I am not saying for one moment that God caused the Coronavirus, (that knowledge is above my paygrade!), as I lean more towards the theological slant that God often allows and uses these things, without proactively sending them upon us. But I can still clearly see that there is a judgement taking place in the world that is casting a light on many injustices, and as a Church, we should take note.

I find it fascinating that while the world is fighting a viral infection that attacks our breathing, a man dies on the streets of Minneapolis whispering *"I can't breathe"* – his words going on to flood the headlines of our global news. Could it be that the entire world is also suffocating under the brutal knee of hatred, bigotry, sexual perversion, lies, exaggeration, fakery and the pointless pursuit of seedy pleasure? Can you hear God speaking through it all?

Perhaps God is offering the repentant the clear fresh air of a new life in Him? Is the Oxygen of Salvation about to flood the worlds lungs as she cries out to God *"I can't breathe!"*? God's judgement is always redemptive in purpose, so I believe He will indeed respond as we cry out to Him. And the Church should lead the way.

Judgement Closer To Home

The Church should take note of this season not simply because we are observers of God's acts of judgement in the world, but because we are far from *"without sin"* ourselves. Judgement often *"begins with God's own House"* (1 Peter 4:17), so we must ask *"What is God saying to the Church about His judgment in this time?"*

Of course, I'm sure that most of you reading this book are not cruel dictators, running a sex trafficking ring or oppressing the poor (though I would invite us to question whether we are more bigoted, racist or indifferent to the poor than we'd like to admit?). I think God's judgment is being revealed to the Church, unveiling some areas of sin that are very unique to the Christian, as a purifying time for us to get ready for what He is about to do next.

For some months I have felt God calling the Church, especially leaders, back into what I informally call the "Strategy Rooms of Heaven" – God has new methods and purposes to unveil to us, and He wants to cleanse and prepare us for those new days.

On the 16th April 2020, when praying about a new spirit of innovation that I feel is about to flood the Church (I'll come back to that later, I promise!) I felt God say *"Remember the greatest innovation is about **WHO YOU ARE**, not **WHAT YOU DO!** I am dealing with idolatry, drawing you to deeper intimacy, and that will lead to clear identity – from that will flow fresh innovation and purpose."*

Wow! It's so easy in these times when we are searching for new ways, better days, and great adventures in God, that we can miss the simple reality that God wants to develop WHO we are more than WHAT we do!

I may be fifty years down the road, and I've spent many of those following God the best I can, but He's still more interested in me becoming like Christ, than in me being a success. You might want to read that last phrase again, slowly.

Early in 2020 I prophetically, but quite vividly, "heard" the clanging of hammer on anvil deep within my soul, a strange occurrence I've never had before or since! God said *"I am forming steel like strength within you – FORMATION is more important than FULFILMENT. Stop trying to RUSH to fulfilment and give yourself to FORMATION. Deep, inner, purity, intimacy, authenticity and strength."*

I believe there are several things, common to many in the Body of Christ, that God is dealing with, and these are going to mark this new era in a profound way.

God is dealing with…

1. Empire Building, Branding and Competition

"God opposes the proud but shows favour to the humble." James 4:6

I believe it grieves the heart of God that many of us build churches and ministries and view them as our own, and perhaps even as in competition to each other. He hates it that we fail to truly celebrate each other's successes and secretly smile at each other's failings. How do I know this happens? Because it happens in me!

I believe the Church of the new era is going to be one that ends its personal empire building, the obsession about how many members we have, how big our attendance is, or how many churches commit to our denomination. It's time for our self-obsessed branding and self-promotion to end. Can we simply make something great of the Name of JESUS? A One Church, One Lord, One Body, glorious Bride is about to arise, where it won't matter who gets the numbers, whose brand is better or who's got the slicker website. We are one.

We will start to behave as one family and one team, across entire cities and nations. More and more churches will find humble ways to brand themselves as simply "The Body of Christ" – one part of an amazing family across a region or beyond. High church, low church and every style in between must start to truly love each other. Large churches and small fellowships will work together. Generosity will be our light, merciful love our language and family our atmosphere. We must jettison suspicion, gossip and one-upmanship. Stop trying to build monuments to our own greatness and begin to surrender to the name of Christ. It's time!

2. Envy, Jealously and Comparison

"But by the grace of God I am what I am, and his grace to me was not without effect." 1 Corinthians 15:10

To continue, the only way to become free from the self-obsessed culture outlined in point 1, which has marked church leadership for decades, is to embrace radical humility. We must become content to play our part, without denigrating one another. So much envy and judgmentalism is masked by tearing into the minor faults in others, often under the smoke screen of righteous indignation. We nastily accuse the mega-church leader of sheep stealing, thriving on entertainment and having no time for us. The larger church pastors denigrate the small church pastors as out of date, flaky and lazy, "If only they'd update, they'd have bigger numbers" we simplistically assume.

But what if we surrendered to the reality that we only need to be what God has made us to be? More than that, that God positively needs us to remain confidently unique, in order to fulfil a specific purpose, in a specific place, for a specific time.

When Moses responded to the wisdom of his father-in-law Jethro by placing the Children of Israel into tribal groups, each with their own wise leaders, it says,

"He chose capable men from all over Israel and appointed them as leaders over the people. He put them in charge of groups of one thousand, one hundred, fifty, and ten." Exodus 18:25

I believe this verse shows that we all have capabilities and capacities given from heaven, expressed as the capability to care for a *"one thousand, one hundred, fifty, and ten"*. Can you can hear echoes of Jesus Parable of the Talents here, where some are given five Talents (a unit of money), some two and some one Talent (Matthew 25:14+)?

The lesson in both these passages is that God designates capacity, and it would be unwise to fight any perceived unfairness in that. The truth found here is that the life of a person designed by God to care for ten, is no less valuable than the life created to lead a thousand. Until we can rest in that fact, we will ache under a burden of covetousness.

In my first flush of ministry and leadership in the early 1990's, all my church heroes were mega-church pastors. I loved watching them preach and enjoyed drinking from their ability to communicate the Word of God, captivating congregations of thousands for an hour at a time.

This, of course, affected my development as a young man, as elusive root systems of covetousness, ego and ambition subtlety infiltrated my heart and mind over the years. Unashamedly I wanted to end up in the ranks of the "Great Preachers". At some point I had to ask the honest question *"But what if I'm not meant to be a mega-church pastor, great orator or leader of thousands? Am I going to be grumpy about that, bitter or resentful? Or am I going to rejoice at the size of my God-given capacity, no matter how small? Will I be faithful with the 'Talent' He has given me, or will I bury it, because of a burden of covetousness?"*

Covetousness is so grave it ranks among the "top ten" in God's commandments (Exodus 20:17). Sitting around wishing you were *as famous as ….* , *had as many social media followers as … , had as much income as … , or led a church as big as …,* is a powerful drug that will bend you towards bitterness if you're not careful. It will highjack your soul and shipwreck your destiny.

It is time, as the people of God, that we cultivate contentment in our callings, while remaining ambitious for the Kingdom of God. We must love the body of Christ across the world, in all its hues, from the mega-church to the small prophetic house. We must see that some are made to be large "regiments" in God's army, while others are smaller "Special Forces" teams. Each are unique and so valuable, as each reaches a certain people group, and each create distinctive discipleship opportunities for the participants.

Let's repent of covetousness and start enjoying the gloriously exclusive journey God has placed each of us on. Let's end the *copy and pasting* of methods and brands, and fully enter the landscape of promise God has distinctly placed before each of us. Great, unique, joy-filled adventures await us there.

3.   Compromise

"Repent, then, and turn to God, so that your sins may be wiped out, that times of refreshing may come from the Lord." Acts 3:19

Into the heart of weary or disappointed souls often comes compromise. Secret sins, fallen thought-lives, habits that attempt to mask the monotony of ministry – these eat at the very roots of our energy, and in this Great Pause God is speaking words of challenge, love, forgiveness and comfort into every dark corner of our beings. It is time to reassess, to be honest with God, to repent to a friend, and to draw grace down into our souls more deeply once again.

"Those who cleanse themselves from the latter will be instruments for special purposes, made holy, useful to the Master and prepared to do any good work." 2 Timothy 2:21

"Embarrass sin before it embarrasses you" I quoted in my book

"Stronger", a helpful line from Jesse Duplantis. The consequence of sin sometimes has a delayed reaction to it, and so we can think we are getting away with things we know we simply should not do. While in public we appear to be godly and on fire, our private lives can be dark, mirky under-worlds of secret failure or addictive, unhealthy coping mechanisms. But eventually, when sin is *"fully grown"* (James 1:15), we always finally reap from what we've sown (Galatians 6:7) and our failures are unveiled. Far better to repent early, cry out for grace, get some help if needed, and deal with our inconsistencies as openly and aggressively as possible, that we would be set apart for God's most noble work.

4.   Weariness of Soul

"Are you tired? Worn out? Burned out on religion? Come to me. Get away with me and you'll recover your life. I'll show you how to take a real rest. Walk with me and work with me— watch how I do it. Learn the unforced rhythms of grace. I won't lay anything heavy or ill-fitting on you. Keep company with me and you'll learn to live freely be and lightly." Matthew 11:28030 (The Message)

Many in leadership, and many in the ranks of every Church, are deeply weary at a soul level. Some lives are so filled with busyness and burden that we have lost connection with the sounds of our own souls, and it is this that has led to private compromise. But I believe a deep healing of soul is being released from heaven. Burdens that have trapped leaders in certain unhealthy "soothing" behaviours, are being lifted away, like Saul's armour was lifted off David (1 Samuel 17:39).

"Hope deferred makes the heart sick, but a longing fulfilled is a tree of life." Proverbs 13:12

Sometimes the long period of waiting for fulfilment wearies our souls, and makes us heart-sick. But I believe disappointment is about to be replaced by fulfilment, even though in many cases I believe we are going to be surprised at the unusual ways God fulfils the desires of our hearts in this new era!

May long term illness crumble under the weight of God's healing power, may depression lift, sick souls be washed in wonder once again and may God reward many of you who have endured the onslaught of the enemy for several years. God is about to give you recompense, restitution, restoration and redemption. He will *"restore the years the locust has eaten!"* (Joel 2:25).

Leader, God wants your soul healthy, breathing deeply of the fresh air of heaven, not succumbing to the claustrophobic demands of disappointment or historic tradition. A rested soul is a soul that can joy at other's success, truly grieve at others losses, and strike out into new territory, free from cynicism and avoidance. So seek Him in prayer, in worship, in the Word and in joyful intimacy, for there is a refreshing over-haul of your soul about to take place!

5.   The Worship of Method above Intimacy

"Isaiah was right when he prophesied about you hypocrites; as it is written: "'These people honour me with their lips, but their hearts are far from me. They worship me in vain; their teachings are merely human rules.' You have let go of the commands of God and are holding on to human traditions." Mark 7:5-8

It is possible for us to talk about Jesus but have a heart that is far from God. We so easily set up camp in old methods, favourite styles and enjoyable expressions of our faith, but that doesn't mean God is actually in them anymore. Corrie Ten Boom once said *"It hurts when God has to PRY things out of our hands"* and I feel that is exactly what God has been doing in this extraordinary pivoting pit-stop time.

At Easter in 2020 I felt led to read through all the resurrection stories in all four Gospels once again. I was deeply impacted by the obvious, yet powerful fact that they looked for Jesus where they last put him, *but He was not there anymore!*

"On the first day of the week, very early in the morning, the women took the spices they had prepared and went to the tomb. They found the stone rolled away from the tomb, but

when they entered, they did not find the body of the Lord Jesus. While they were wondering about this, suddenly two men in clothes that gleamed like lightning stood beside them. In their fright the women bowed down with their faces to the ground, but the men said to them, 'Why do you look for the living among the dead?" Luke 24:1-5

In this time of Divine Reset, God is smashing through our religious spirits, attitudes and man-made formations, revealing the bankruptcy of the faith of many. We worship historic moments and methods, but we need to learn that GOD MOVES ON. He will not stay where you last found Him, or where He met you last year, or last century, or even last week! – HE MOVES ON! And we must move on with Him!

"Why do you look for the living among the dead" said the angels *"HE IS NOT HERE!"* (Luke 24:6). Just because God is the same yesterday, today and forever, doesn't mean He does the same things, and uses the same methods yesterday, today and forever. HE MOVES ON!

Be prepared to be driven by God to a new place of ministry, method and intimate encounter as you enter this new era. The old patterns of our history are not entwined enough with God's contemporary purposes to bring about the revival He desires. We must stop seeking ministry and start seeking Him. Stop hungering for a reiteration of the past, and deeply desire to go from glory to glory. Let's end the impotent repetition of religious tradition and find the imminent voice of God found in His powerful presence. If we stop worshipping method, and instead live from intimacy, fresh streams of salvation will flow on barren heights – and these heights will become the land of the new era in which we will glory.

Whether it is justice in the world for the oppressed and the forgotten, or a time of judgement and preparation for the Church, we must give ourselves in this time to the formations, the challenges, to the probing convictions of heaven. Out of it will come rivers of grace, on the banks of which will form trees of fruitfulness, a blessing to the nations around us!

Give yourself to personal repentance and holiness. Then give yourself to the call of taking the Gospel to the poor, the down-trodden and those with no voices. If we do such a thing, we may just find ourselves emerging as the image of Jesus in the world, that His glory may fill the earth for all to see.

JOURNAL & SESSION 3 DISCUSSION TIME

Use the questions below to ponder and journal, or to discuss this chapter with your small group or team.

1. Judgement is all over the pages of scripture but is quite controversial today. Why do you think that might be?

2. What might God be saying to us through the death of George Floyd and the subsequent racial unrest around the world?

3. Can you see any other evidence of God's judgment in the world at present?

4. Can you identify any areas of divine discipline taking place in your church community right now? How could you further co-operate with God as He develops you?

5. Take the 5 areas of judgment listed in this chapter and discuss/journal how you think you're doing. Try to be brutally honest, repentant and gracious with each other! The areas are *1) Empire Building, Branding and Competition (Pride). 2) Envy, Jealousy and Comparison. 3) Compromise (Sin). 4) Weariness of Soul (Poor self-management). 5) Placing Method above Intimacy (religiosity).*

JOURNAL

JOURNAL

A RETURN TO THE PRAYER ROOMS

8

The Lord says...

"I am calling my people back to the Prayer Rooms in droves in this season, to encounter my presence and thus release my glory among you. My jealousy for your intimacy is calling out to your heart! And from that undistracted place will flow waves of outpouring, releasing miraculous power and the amplification of my voice in your heart. Dreams, visions, encounters, visitations and manifestations will become increasingly common place for you, as I gradually raise the intensity of my presence among you. You are to be found in my Strategy Rooms receiving fresh blueprints for this season, forsaking old methods, and embracing new grace and mantles prepared long ago for you."

Chapter 8
A Return To The Prayer Rooms

"The early church had no buildings, vision planning, money, or political influence. They were shunned, shamed, and persecuted. But they turned the world upside down because of an absolute dependence upon the Holy Spirit and the preaching of the gospel." - Phillip Nation

On the 23rd February 2019, whilst seeking God regarding Brexit, the phenomenon of the United Kingdom's decision to distance itself from the legal, political and financial infrastructure of the European Union, I sensed God speaking into Great Britain's political upheaval. I am by no means signalling here whether I am a "Leaver" or "Remainer" from this word, (as it's a very contentious position to declare publicly in the UK), and in fact, I was accused by both sides of being a spokesperson for the other!

But here is what I received from God, and I share it with you here because it became more a prophetic word about prayer at this pivotal time, than about Brexit:

"I saw Great Britain as a tree that once stood alone, but was now hidden among a great forest of many trees, having lost its distinction and unique purpose. Quite literally, for many in the public and many in power, there was little clarity, and a loss of true purpose under the dark, damp overgrown canopy created by the large forest.

But then change stirred. There was a shifting in the landscape, a splintering, a small but ultimately seismic shift, that brought about a definite divine change: While Britain did not stand completely alone, there was enough change in the branches around about and enough adjustment in the landscape to allow her distinct shape and purpose to be seen. Then I noticed that as the branches in the canopy of the forest had shifted, a new wave of sunlight hit the ground around her for the first time in a long time, and new life began to burst forth.

I believe God is saying, that while the political shifts that will take place over the next months and years will not bring about the clear and full political extreme "breakaway" that some have desired, a greater shift has indeed taken place in the heavenlies, throwing fresh light and fresh purpose, and a new surge of power from heaven will touch the land. There will become just enough distinction in the heavenlies over Great Britain for her divine purpose to be re-ignited.

As the fresh sunlight hits the ground and the heavenly landscape adjusts, I see it is as though a divine defibrillator is at work, stirring the Church in the nation once again. As sunlight warms the earth, seeds of ancient purpose, revivals and the prayers of saints over centuries begin to warm, and the ground itself begins to stir…

A Fresh Uprising of Prayer

A fresh uprising, a surge of prayer, worship, praise and prophetic intercession is about to burst through the veins of the Church in Great Britain, brought by heaven itself. Meetings large and small, to worship, encounter and pray, will begin to build a new kind of canopy, a canopy of praise, that heaven's kingdom will rest upon. Thousands of small prayer meetings, in cities and villages across the nation, will draw heaven near in this time. The King desires to be "enthroned on the praises of His people!" and He is preparing the heavens over Great Britain for His arrival!

Many have thought worship has already been renewed in recent decades, but a fresh uprising is about to take worshippers to a whole new level- It will be like heaven on earth at times.

In this time, do not look to the corridors of Parliament for powerful changes in the nation, but look to the closets of the praying. The Church is the heart of power in the nation and the nations, and a fresh wave of prayer is about to sweep over the land. This uprising of prayer will lead to power – power among the saints on the streets, in workplaces, in communities and in places of influence, in ways many have never seen nor imagined before. The healing touch of heaven will be magnified in power as the Church prays and worships.

For Such a Time As This

Where many have "dug ditches," creating channels of influence into communities over years through social action and community engagement, and yet have become disappointed at the lack of Kingdom results, they will realise they have been digging "For such a time as this". Many inroads of influence into communities, the poor and the many spheres of influence in the nation, local and national, will become irrigation channels, filled with the prayers and the powers of a new season of heaven coming upon the nation. Many will realise they had been preparing the land "for such a time as this."

As Britain attempts to readjust its position in Europe, there will also be a fresh uprising of compassion for mainland Europe, resulting in new waves of missionaries from Britain to the mainland, carrying this fresh prayer and power to community after community. I even see many that have travelled from African nations to the U.K. will also find themselves moving into mainland Europe. A compassionate move of missions, fuelled by prayer and armed with heavens power, is about to stir across the new landscape of Great Britain and Europe.

While many will complain that there are still too many political entanglements with Europe in the coming years, enough of a divine shift in the heavens will have taken place to release God's divine sunlight on Great Britain. Focus on the fresh light shining from the heavens in this season, rather than the problematic purposes of man. There is a Greater divine work taking place than can ever be wrought by the human corridors of power.

Pray with me – "Father, Your Kingdom Come, Your will be done…in Great Britain, as it is in heaven!" (1)

A Return To Prayer

In Acts 2 it states the early disciples were devoted to several things (Please note, they "devoted themselves", there was no 12 step programme to try to get them to commit – Oh leader, don't you dream of that day?!).

"They devoted themselves to the apostles' teaching and to fellowship, to the breaking of bread and to prayer. Everyone was filled with awe at the many wonders and signs performed by the apostles. All the believers were together and had everything in common. They sold property and possessions to give to anyone who had need. Every day they continued to meet together in the temple courts. They broke bread in their homes and ate together with glad and sincere hearts, praising God and enjoying the favour of all the people. And the Lord added to their number daily those who were being saved." Acts 2:42-47

It seems they were devoted to good teaching from the apostles, fellowship (A good old word for friendship), the breaking of bread and prayer. The results were amazing, miraculous, generous and joyous, with *"God adding daily to their number those being saved"* (verse 47).

Now I want you to compare that description of the early church, to your church:

Imagine if you will, that an alien landed among our western churches today, and observed what we were most devoted to. Would the list be the same?

Let me be cheeky here… I suspect it may read something more like *"The western Church devoted themselves to Sunday services, singing songs, churches with good youth groups, kids work, smart buildings, free parking and, er, good coffee!"*

During the Great Pause of 2020 I have repeatedly analysed all the activities of Revive Church, evaluating them for fruitfulness, signs of life and measurable impact. I have also assessed the state of my own weary soul, asking the question, "Is this it?" If I'm honest, the lives impacted have been smaller than I'd like, and yet I'm also so very weary from doing good. Many leaders like me are tired. Deep down, dog-tired.

I have begun to ask profound questions of my own soul and my own leadership (and my staff!). What would Jesus really do in our region, in this time? If we were to start again, what would we do differently? Does it feel like we're on an adventure with Jesus? If money wasn't a problem, and fear didn't exist, what would we do differently? Who are we really becoming? Are we a good testament to the joy, power and compassion of the Kingdom of God?

The other great question I have asked is *"Are the main things that marked out the early Church, truly the main thing in our church today?"* Do we pray like they prayed, devote like they devoted, hang out like they would hang out and give like they gave? Are we the real deal, or has mission drift and western consumerism hijacked our culture?

Love God, Love Others

When asked to define the very core of the Law, Jesus words presumably shocked the rule-laden religious leaders, who were probably so lost in a blizzard of small print, they would have found it virtually impossible to summarise what truly matters most. That's what religion does to you!

Out of hundreds of rules and supposed pressing traditions, Jesus cut through the demanding entanglements of religion and summed up God's purpose for us in a mere 24 words:

*"Teacher, which is the greatest commandment in the Law?" Jesus replied: "***'Love the Lord your God with all your heart and with all your soul and with all your mind.'*** This is the first and greatest commandment. And the second is like it:* ***'Love your neighbour as yourself.'*** Matthew 22:36-40

He did such an awesome job of simplifying what's most important, that I think I can now crystalise it down even more, to perhaps just four words:

Love God, Love Others.

That's it!

I mean, doesn't that also sum up the passage in Acts 2, describing the early Church so ablaze with heavens priorities? They devoted themselves to God, to each other, and to the world. That's all we're here to do!

I have sat and conducted many an appraisal of a minister, staff member or project leader, and seldom have I heard the simple question that should be ranked above every other in Jesus estimation:

"Do you love God? I mean are you absolutely sold out in devotion to Him?" quickly followed by *"Do you completely love the people you're serving?"*

Do you love Jesus? Are you rabidly, passionately, craving His presence? When is the last time your love for Him drove you to pray all night? How much time do you spend with Him each day? Do you adore His Word, crave His voice, surrender to His merest whim and willingly sacrifice to please Him?

And do you really love the people He's given you? Do you even like, let alone love, your neighbour? Do you love them, or just chat to them occasionally? Do you LOVE the city where He's placed you? Would you give your life for it just as He gave His life for you? Do you love your church family, or is it all about the work, the projects, the ministry and the accomplishments?

It's so easy to start out loving Jesus, but then ministry has a way of wearing you down, until you become a full-time minister, but a part-time lover of Jesus. There was a time you would pray all night, devour the Bible, give all of your worldly wealth away, and do anything to spend a little more time with Him. But then we slowly fall for the accolades of success, or get wrapped up in the bitterness of betrayals, the weariness of work, become side-lined by offences or the disappointment of failure. We might love the platform, love expressing our giftings, or even feed off the joy of being needed by others – but is that really loving God and loving others?

If loving God is the start point of our entire lives and ministries, then I want to put before you that we need to get back to spending time with Jesus, just for the sake of loving Him and enjoying Him.

Would it be possible to get away from the bustle and complexity of what Church has become for many, and simply get back to voice of God? Are there things we could prune away from the busyness of church life, to help us get back to the voice, the intimacy and the harvest that God intended?

Just Two Things Matter

As I pondered my way radically through my busy list of Revive Church activities and aims, I eventually landed on just two things that seemed to matter in the light of this Acts 2 passage. Remarkably these two things are perfectly aligned with Jesus call to *Love God and Love Others*. If we could just find the energy and space to devote ourselves to these two properly, we might just have a revival on our hands.

As I assessed my life, and all that our busy church does, only two things were truly significant:

I believe we should be devoted to *prayer* and *mission*.

You could say we should give ourselves to *encounter* and *evangelism*. Perhaps a better phrase is that we should lose ourselves in *worship* and devote ourselves to *justice*. Maybe we should build churches around *seeking* and *sending*, or *intimacy* and *assignment*. Or call it *being with The One* and letting His *Kingdom Come*. Whatever your favourite phrase, only two things seem to truly matter with eternal consequence, *Love God, Love Others*. Be found near Him, in continual personal fellowship, then *"Go into all the world"* and reach more people with the Gospel.

Many will say, *"But what about discipleship?"* and I agree, we need to be equipping, training and maturing believers. But in my personal experience, teaching and training can often take over and we fill our church programmes with courses, small cosy growth groups and teaching times. Perhaps Biblical discipleship would be better placed as something we do *as we pray together and as we go together?* God never meant us to spend our lives in a classroom, but rather in prayer and on a mission.

For most, I do wonder if we teach and train so much, that we use up all our free time, budget and energy on knowledge, instead of mission? Somehow, we have to prune our church lives down until *we fully pray, and fully go.*

A House Of Prayer For All Nations

First then, let's talk a little about the call of God for a new move of prayer among us. If we are honest, the prayer meeting is usually one of least attended activities in church. It seems many Christians would rather do most other things in church life, than pray. And yet it sits there, firmly in the list of things the early church was most *devoted* to.

As I have gone through our months of pondering and seeking God for a way forward this year, I would say that our church family, Revive (and perhaps yours will be the same, but no pressure!) is awash with church services, ablaze with discipleship opportunities and we have teaching times coming out of our ears. But as we enter the new season, I feel a need to redefine ourselves under the banner that Jesus raised when He described His House:

"Then they came to Jerusalem. And He entered the temple area and began to drive out those who were selling and buying on the temple grounds, and He overturned the tables of the money changers and the seats of those who were selling doves; and He would not allow anyone to carry merchandise through the temple grounds. And He began to teach and say to them, "Is it not written: 'MY HOUSE WILL BE CALLED A HOUSE OF PRAYER FOR ALL THE NATIONS'? But you have made it a DEN OF ROBBERS." Mark 11:15-17

Through this powerful and passionate moment in the short

ministry of Jesus, we see His longing, His priority, His fiercely jealous purpose for us, that the House of God should be *"A House of Prayer for all nations"*.

So the question I ask of my church, and you should ask of yours is, *Can I really describe our church primarily as a House of Prayer?*

If a "secret shopper" hid among us, would they list prayer at the top of our review? Would it even make the top three? Would he or she be amazed at our ardent, passionate, unstifled LOVE for God? Would they find us fanatical about Jesus, lost in prayer, abandoned to His presence? Would they say *"It was like I had strayed into the book of Acts?"*

If Jesus was that secret shopper, would He turn over tables with disgusted zeal at what we have made the church, or dance with delight at the passionate worship, the continual prayer and our abandoned devotion?

Undistracted

In Dr. Brian Simmon's beautiful rendition of Jesus' visit to Martha and Mary's home, his Passion Translation of the Bible states:

"As Jesus and the disciples continued on their journey, they came to a village where a woman welcomed Jesus into her home. Her name was Martha and she had a sister named Mary. Mary sat down attentively before the Master, absorbing every revelation he shared. But Martha became exasperated by finishing the numerous household chores in preparation for her guests, so she interrupted Jesus and said, "Lord, don't you think it's unfair that my sister left me to do all the work by myself? You should tell her to get up and help me."

The Lord answered her, "Martha, my beloved Martha. Why are you upset and troubled, pulled away by all these many distractions? Are they really that important? Mary has discovered the one thing most important by choosing to sit at my feet. She is undistracted, and I won't take this privilege from her." Luke 10:38-42

We need to rediscover what it means to be **undistracted**. To redesign our churches and lives to give ourselves to the "most important thing" – Sitting *"down attentively before the Master, absorbing every revelation he"* shares.

Recently, as part of a journaling exercise, I began to note on a large flipchart, every miracle or evidence of God's Kingdom coming that I had ever seen in my own life. With small scribbles I listed down along half a dozen columns, miracle after miracle. From miraculous provision, to uncannily accurate prophecies, from legs growing several inches, to open visions, emptied wheelchairs and lives saved. Even the B.B.C. had reported some of the miracles, while other TV Crews found themselves healed as they visited our church!

With two thirds of the large flip chart sheet filled, I was deeply encouraged and reminded of many of the things God had done for me. Next, I pondered what to do with the empty third of my large sheet of paper. After a few moments considering, I chose to begin listing every period of remarkable encounter, extended times of prayer and fasting, seasons of focussed intercession and prolonged times of giving myself privately to God's presence.

As the paper began filling out with amazing headlines from dedicated times of seeking of God's face and favour, a pattern began to emerge before me on the page. Each time of deeper devotion on the bottom third of my flipchart paper, had resulted in the greater manifestations of the Kingdom on the top half of my sheet. Greater encounters had repeatedly led to greater expressions of God. Each miracle season had been pre-empted by a choice to dig deeper into God through prayer.

How thick had I been?! It's simple, it's biblical, it's obvious. Pray more, and more stuff happens!

As my friend Ian Christensen often says *"Much prayer, much power. Little prayer, little power. No prayer, ..."*

He usually leaves the congregation to fill in the final blank.

It now seemed obvious to me that that the times God's miracle power had been released, had been preceded and under-girded by a particularly undiluted focus in prayer, listening, worship, fasting, seeking and soaking in Him. It's as if the *"One Thing"* of being in God's presence, actually leads to the *"Many Things"* of the Kingdom coming among us.

Maybe that's partly what Jesus means when He stated, *"Seek first his kingdom and his righteousness, and all these things will be given to you as well."* (Matthew 6:33). Certainly His teachings on prayer encourage us to call out *"Your Kingdom come, your will be done"* (Matthew 6:10) presumably because more will happen when we do!

As evangelist J. John always says, *"When I pray, coincidences happen!"*

From Prayer Rooms To Glory Rooms

Could it be that our propensity to run to mission and busyness, without attentively tending to our altars of prayer, means much of our church efforts are often powerless good works? Does our prayerlessness mean we lack the markers of God's power among us, His presence upon us and His glory within us?

But what if we take this Divine Reset as a signal to return to our makers instructions, that we should be a House of Prayer for all nations? To passionately love God first, before we busy ourselves with anything else. To give ourselves in undistracted ways to His presence and loveliness, to wait on His words, to gaze on His beauty.

I believe it would transform the very atmosphere of our church families if we did! To begin with, rather than the mere enthusiasm caused by an exciting vision or great communicator, the Church would instead find a far more divine atmosphere begins to live powerfully among us, the very glory of God!

In my book "500" I prophesied about an increasing sense of glory being poured into the Church in the coming new era. This, I believe, is the environment a Church devoted to prayer will begin to enjoy:

"The Church will be filled with glory. A weighty sense of presence that has grown since the early 1900's will begin to flood every corner of the Church – even the most stoic of church expressions will be found weeping at the wonder of His goodness again. Of course, there will be a backlash, that the coming glory is a figment of overly excited "Charismatic" imaginations, but the rising tide of glory and power will reach everyone who is thirsty – the coming move will be so obviously brought by the hand of heaven, that most of the Church will eventually open itself to new realms of power.

Signs and wonders will become incredibly common place – even among children and denominations formerly thought of as "dead". Indeed the dead will be raised, remarkable healings and miracles, transfigurations, men and women glowing at the presence of God. These signs will fascinate the world and eventually be impossible to ignore, even by the most wary of media outlets." (2)

The Distinguishing Presence

In Moses' encountering of God's glory, he seemed to persuade the apparently reluctant Deity to travel with them for their journey to the Promised Land. In the passage that recounts this story, we find an unusual phrase that I believe cuts to the heart of how a church should feel, and it challenges me to the core.

*Then Moses said to him, "If your Presence does not go with us, do not send us up from here. How will anyone know that you are pleased with me and with your people unless you go with us? **What else will distinguish me and your people from all the other people on the face of the earth?"***

And the LORD said to Moses, "I will do the very thing you have asked, because I am pleased with you and I know you by name." Exodus 33:14-17 (Emphasis added).

The line that always gets me in this passage is the phrase "What else will distinguish me and your people from all the other peo-

ple on the face of the earth?"

It is the very presence and glory of God among the Church that distinguishes us, marks us out and makes us different. We are not a mere club, with a bit of singing, moral lecturing and good works on the side. We are supposed to be the very House of the Living God, the Body of Christ (1 Timothy 3:15), the place where His glory dwells (Psalm 26:8).

Until we give ourselves fully to the focus of prayer, deep worship and encounter, I fear we will be dry, bankrupt versions of the real thing. We may be busy about our good works, but we will be devoid of power, Spirit-filled in name only, seeing little or none of God's miraculous power from decade to decade.

How might you become a House of Prayer for all nations? How should you respond to the call to become "undistracted" in your love for God? How might your church find itself fulfilling the original cultural design of God's church by having "prayer" listed among your highest priorities? I'm sure it will be outworked uniquely with each of us, but if we do find ways to become House of Prayer and encounter, then I'm convinced God's glory will flood us.

Once filled with God's glory and presence, I believe we will have something powerful to offer the world, as we head to the second great priority of the God-designed Church – *Love Others…*

A New Heart For Harvest

I believe most church families don't have enough time or energy in their margins to truly focus on prayer. We are diluted and thin, aiming at too many major emphases at one time. As we become busy, and different pressures demand platform, resources and leadership focus, we often find ourselves doing many things, but not the top two priorities - *"Love God, Love Others"* with the concentration they require to have a powerful effect.

But if we truly return to the Prayer Rooms of our churches, I believe it will lead to an explosion of mission, both local and global. Once a life has been touched by God's glory in the prayer rooms of a church, you cannot help but be moved by what moves God, the plight of the lost, the poor, the prisoner and the prodigal.

Out from the place of encounter will come a generation like Isaiah saying *"Here I am, send me!"* (Isaiah 6:8) as we discover innovative ways to reach new souls, disciple new nations and people groups, love our neighbours and keep evangelism passionately to the front and fore of our church plans and passions.

But in the era to come I also sense a mandate not only for evangelism, but for Kingdom Come, the complete transformation of society and the *"restoration of all things"* (Acts 3:21) as promised. That is why I believe part of God's Divine Reset for the Church is not only to encounter Him afresh in the prayer rooms of heaven, and to come out passionate about harvest and souls, but also, that we would begin to be challenged to invade and subdue our world with God's kindness and goodness as we *Love Others* in His power.

Here's what I mean…

Sources
1. https://jarrodcooper.net/2019/02/23/prophetic-word-regarding-great-britain-brexit/
2. https://www.amazon.co.uk/dp/B075ZXP694/ref=dp-kindle-redirect?_encoding=UTF8&btkr=1

JOURNAL & SESSION 4 DISCUSSION TIME

Use the questions below to ponder and journal, or to discuss this chapter with your small group or team.

1. Describe your own church strengths, with great honesty, in half a dozen statements.

2. How does your own church compare to the description of the early church found in Acts 2:42-47?

3. How could you give yourself to truly *"Love God"* more in your culture, activities, budget, energy and focus? What things get in the way of you doing this more?

4. Discuss/contemplate the challenge of this paragraph from the chapter: *"Do you love Jesus? Are you rabidly, passionately, craving His presence? When is the last time your love for Him drove you to pray all night? How much time do you spend with Him each day? Do you adore His Word, crave His voice, surrender to His merest whim and willingly sacrifice to please Him?"*

5. If it is not, how could your church become a *"House of Prayer for All Nations"*?

6. How could you give yourself to truly *"Love Others"* more in your culture, activities, budget, energy and focus? What things get in the way of you doing this more?

7. Finally, reflect and/or discuss this challenging passage: *"Do you really love the people He's given you? Do you even like, let alone love, your neighbour? Do you love them, or just chat to them occasionally? Do you LOVE the city where He's placed you? Would you give your life for it just as He gave His life for you? Do you love your church family, or is it all about the work, the projects, the ministry and the accomplishments?"*

JOURNAL

JOURNAL

THY KINGDOM COME

The Lord says...

"From the Prayer Rooms and the Strategy Rooms will rise in you an embracing of the Kingdom mandate to "restore all things" (Acts 3:21) like no generation has ever done before. Your hearts will break over the state of your nation, city, neighbours and work colleagues. This is about more than just a harvest, though many souls will be saved. This is about restoration and Kingdom Come. The passion for transformation will begin to stir in you like "a fire shut up in your bones" (Jeremiah 20:9). You will no longer be content to "play church" and waste time on the mere trinkets of Christianity. I am releasing in you a sense of responsibility for your land and for your world because it is time for the re-ordering of all things, until one day you will say "the kingdoms of this world have become the kingdoms of our God" (Revelation 11:15)."

Chapter 9
Thy Kingdom Come

"The Kingdom of God is not a matter of getting individuals to heaven, but of transforming the life on earth into the harmony of heaven." - Walter Rauschenbusch

As the Church simplifies to get back it's devotion to prayer and divine encounter, I believe the result will be an explosive harvest of souls, but not only that, a full embracing of the mandate that the Church has been given, to see the Kingdom come on the earth.

The Kingdom is not the same thing as the Church. While the concept of the Church is how we gather, the concept of the Kingdom is how God reigns on the earth, through His saints.

In simple terms, the idea of the Church comes from the Greek word ekklesia, meaning "to call out", a wording eventually replaced for us by common words like "assembly" or "congregation." Put simply, Church is the "called out ones" gathering together as an assembly. But the influence of that assembly of holy ones is to reach beyond their walls and touch the world.

The Kingdom is wider and broader than the gathered Church. It speaks of entire cultures coming under the influence and blessing of God, flowing through the "salt and light" (Matthew 5:13-16) presence of the "Ekklesia" believers throughout society. (1a)

Probably Jesus primary definition of the nature and modus operandi of the Kingdom is found in Matthew chapter 13. I want to take the time to take you through this amazing chapter and dwell on a few headlines about how the Kingdom operates and how it is subtly different to the Church.

The Parable Of The Weeds

"Jesus told them another parable: "The kingdom of heaven is like a man who sowed good seed in his field. But while everyone was sleeping, his enemy came and sowed weeds among the wheat, and went away. When the wheat sprouted and formed heads, then the weeds also appeared.

"The owner's servants came to him and said, 'Sir, didn't you sow good seed in your field? Where then did the weeds come from?'

"'An enemy did this,' he replied.

"The servants asked him, 'Do you want us to go and pull them up?'

"'No,' he answered, 'because while you are pulling the weeds, you may uproot the wheat with them. Let both grow together until the harvest. At that time I will tell the harvesters: First collect the weeds and tie them in bundles to be burned; then gather the wheat and bring it into my barn.'" Matthew 13: 24-30

Later in the chapter Jesus explains the Parable of the Weeds:

"Then he left the crowd and went into the house. His disciples came to him and said, "Explain to us the parable of the weeds in the field."

He answered, "The one who sowed the good seed is the Son of Man. The field is the world, and the good seed stands for the people of the kingdom. The weeds are the people of the evil one, and the enemy who sows them is the devil. The harvest is the end of the age, and the harvesters are angels.

"As the weeds are pulled up and burned in the fire, so it will be at the end of the age. The Son of Man will send out his angels, and they will weed out of his kingdom everything that causes sin and all who do evil. They will throw them into the blazing furnace, where there will be weeping and gnashing of teeth.

Then the righteous will shine like the sun in the kingdom of their Father. Whoever has ears, let them hear." Matthew 13:36-43

In the Parable of the Weeds, we find the key difference between "Kingdom" and "Church" clarified. In the New Testament writings about the Church it is clear that purity, dealing thoroughly with sin, and even utilising church discipline are issues to take seriously, the apostle Paul even recommending that a church *"expel the immoral brother"* when needed (1 Corinthians 5:13).

The Body of Christ, the Church, should be a joyfully holy place that accepts sinners. But it is also expected that maturing believers should show the fruits of repentance and be humble and willing to change. This is the House of God, the Ekklessia, the "Called out ones." In the Church we accept discipline because we are disciples. There are standards of holy behaviour that still matter deeply to God, and that God speaks of in intricate detail even in the New Testament epistles.

But the idea of the Kingdom of God is slightly different. While the Church is a home for developing holiness, the Kingdom is about the rule, the reign and the influence of God in an otherwise broken society. While the Church has a need to deal with sinfulness and thoroughly disciple members towards godly lives, the Kingdom of God is more like a field where the righteous and the unrighteous cohabit. It's a messy field with both unholy weeds and virtuous wheat growing side by side. Some religious Christians would want to rip out the wicked weeds on day one, fearful of catching an infection of evil! But if you try to turn the places of Kingdom influence, into mini "Churches", you'll miss the wonder of God's grace and the plans of heaven for the Kingdom to come into every sphere of society!

It is wrong to expect places of mere Kingdom influence, to be like churches in their holy standards. It is equally wrong to expect churches to allow compromise in the morality and actions of its mature believers, those supposed to be "called out" and holy. The Church then, is the place of discipline, discipleship and maturation. But the Kingdom is the influence of that Church beyond her gathered boundaries, lavishing revitalising mercy and restorative grace on a broken world. Let's never mix the two up.

On August 16 1977, when I was just seven years old, one of the greatest singers and performers of a generation died. While millions mourned him around the world, far less truly understood the struggle that had taken place in his tormented soul.

While this spectacular and talented performer was known by the world for his music, the reality is that he was also a deep lover of God. He was a man who evidently wanted to live for Jesus, but in many ways was deeply flawed, and the Church of the day struggled to know what to do with such a mix of talent and brokenness.

You could say that the only way the Church knew how to deal with the "weed-like" life of a sinful, broken pop-star, was to pull up the weeds of wickedness first! Pastors of the era were not able to give the grace to allow the weeds and wheat to grow together for a while, and the result was a tormented soul, who longed for God, but could not find Kingdom grace flowing from the Church.

Ostracised from Church the a-list star would gather renowned celebrities around his piano and sing songs like *"There's a sweet, sweet Spirit in this place, and I know it is the Spirit of the Lord"* as tears ran down their faces. His backing group claimed he moved in what we would today call "words of knowledge" as he seemed, on occasion, to know things by supernatural means. He prayed for his cancer-stricken backing vocalist who was healed! He read the bible each night. [1]

That man was, of course, Elvis Presley.

Footage of Elvis singing his favourite hymn "How Great Thou Art" is legendary and common place, but less noted are the times he would pause to speak to fans carrying "Elvis is the King" banners, and remind them "No, Jesus is the King, I'm just a singer!"

Elvis was a classic mix of broken humanity and beautiful divinity colliding in a person's soul. The Church demanded good behaviour first, and the Kingdom of grace never seemed to reach him.

Sadly, it would appear he never seemed to find out how to bring the two together; how to make peace between his gifts, his talents, his brokenness, the divine grace of God and the demands of a religious church. And as I'm sure you know, his life was difficult and painful, some reporting that by the end of his life, Elvis had "suffered from multiple ailments: glaucoma, high blood pressure, liver damage, and an enlarged colon, each magnified—and possibly caused—by drug abuse." Ultimately, he died of a heart attack. (2)

The night before his death Rick Stanley, who was with him at the time, reported that Elvis prayed "Dear Lord, please show me a way. I'm tired and confused, and I need your help." A few minutes later, Elvis looked at him and said, "Rick, we should all begin to live for Christ." (3)

Isn't it sad that the Church of the day struggled to reach beyond their safe walls of holy behaviour, and never realised this was a chance for the Kingdom to touch the music industry, and perhaps bring a little divine restoration to it? Had the reigning grace of the Kingdom reached out to Elvis and those around him, how different could his story have been?

The demand from churches to "pull out the wickedness" before its time has led to many an aborted advancement for God's Kingdom into a new realm. Instead, we must learn to serve the ungodly, leaving the timings of heaven to bring about deep behavioural change. Like Joseph serving an ungodly pharaoh, or Daniel and his friends blessing idol-worshipping kings from other lands, the Kingdom is about loving the ungodly, and revealing the goodness and kindness of God to environments that don't deserve it, without expecting them to become churches overnight, or ever at all.

Kingdom work is a lot riskier than Church work. It demands we touch the leprous, trusting that we will not become unclean, but instead, our purity will influence and transform society. As we reach out to bless society around us, without the demand that they become just like churches, we will find an amazing favour will rest upon the Church, as summarised in the Parables of the mustard seed and yeast:

The Parables Of The Mustard Seed And The Yeast

"He told them another parable: "The kingdom of heaven is like a mustard seed, which a man took and planted in his field. Though it is the smallest of all seeds, yet when it grows, it is the largest of garden plants and becomes a tree, so that the birds come and perch in its branches."

He told them still another parable: "The kingdom of heaven is like yeast that a woman took and mixed into about sixty pounds of flour until it worked all through the dough." Matthew 13:31-33

My friend Stewart McKinley, a Revive Church kingdom influencer into spheres like medicine, business and education, often speaks of the great influence God has graced his life with by quoting this very passage. He sums it up like this: *"The key truth in these verses is that the Kingdom of God is DISPROPORTIONATE – You do a little, and God makes MUCH of it! That is the power of the Kingdom!"*

Here you find a small mustard seed which would usually produce a small bush, and as one version of the parable puts it in the original language, it become a *"mega-tree"*. It's a totally supernatural and disproportionate occurrence! It shows us that the influence of the Kingdom, through even a small church or faltering believer, can be so huge that the *"birds of the air"* will come to rest in your branches.

I think this means that the people of the world will want to shelter among the people of the Kingdom, as we bless them with what we have to give. They will rest among our kindness, wisdom and sure footedness, as it causes them to feel safe among us. Non-Christian businesses will want to use your conference facilities, employ children from your schools, coffee with you as advisors, enlist your opinions and even speak at their events.

This is the Kingdom coming, and the eventual effect is disproportionate godly influence, as seen in the lives of Joseph and Daniel!

The parable goes on to express the sense of the DISPROPORTIONATE effect of Kingdom activity with the story of the yeast. Yeast is the smallest ingredient in bread, but it has the biggest effect. Just a little yeast transforms the whole loaf with life!

Your mere presence on that school governing board, in that office, in that classroom, or on that planning team can, in time, utterly transform the shape and substance of society as we step out trusting that God's passionate desire for His Kingdom to come among us, will lead to disproportionate blessing on our small actions and investments.

Ultimately, as the Church gives itself to reach the world around us with a Kingdom mindset, this next parable tells us what will happen:

The Parable Of The Net

"Once again, the kingdom of heaven is like a net that was let down into the lake and caught all kinds of fish. When it was full, the fishermen pulled it up on the shore. Then they sat down and collected the good fish in baskets, but threw the bad away. This is how it will be at the end of the age. The angels will come and separate the wicked from the righteous and throw them into the blazing furnace, where there will be weeping and gnashing of teeth." Matthew 13: 47-50

This final thought is that the Kingdom is like a fishing net that is let down over a lake. The lake represents all of society, the good, the bad and the ugly. The Kingdom, then, is a net that covers and reaches out to all.

Imagine that God wants to release a Kingdom net over the whole earth, including the region, nation or city where you feel God has graced you with responsibility. He wants to lay it across entire regions, like my own of Hull & East Yorkshire in northern England. He will lay it over hospitals, businesses, schools and universities, the emergency services, the families, finances and communities of an entire region, as God's desire is to *"restore all things"* (Acts 3:21) in every sphere of society. It is not simply a net of soul-winning evangelism, but also a net of Kingdom influence, restoring entire cultures and spheres of influence back to God.

Notice the Kingdom net will have wicked people under its influence – and they won't be removed until "the end of age", and then by angels:

"The angels will come and separate the wicked from the righteous and throw them into the blazing furnace, where there will be weeping and gnashing of teeth." Matthew 13:50

Yes, some among the wicked who are under the influence of the Kingdom of God, will not be separated out until end of time! Our job therefore, in the context of the Kingdom rather than church discipleship, is not to separate, or remove, or make judgments on people, but rather to subdue them with goodness and kindness, to serve, to advise, to influence and to be salt and light.

We must allow the good, the bad and the ugly to rest in our Kingdom branches. We must influence life and living in disproportionate ways by simply being present and attentive to the needs of society. Slowly, powerfully, the Kingdom will come, and yes, when the Kingdom influence is strong, many more will easily get saved too! But first, we need to give ourselves to taking the Kingdom to every part of society.

As we give ourselves increasingly to Kingdom mission, instead of simply busying ourselves doing churchy things for churchy people, we will begin to realise we are on mission at our places of work, on the streets where we live, at our schools, or even at home – every single day! We are anointed to bring God's goodness and Kingdom in, daily subduing the world through kindness, goodness and love.

Instead of church members existing to serve the pastor (Surely the "top job" in God's organisation we sometimes tend to think) now the pastor and their staff teams exist to serve the schoolteacher, the local councillor, the doctors and nurses, factory workers and business owners. They serve them to help them turn their places of work, family and leisure into landing zones of the Kingdom of God! This is God's plan in this next era of the unfolding of His purposes on earth.

The Seven Mountains Of Influence

In my book "500" I prophesied about the Church's Kingdom mission to what some call the 7-mountains of influence. They are key spheres of influence in society and are places we should focus Kingdom influence, if we hope to eventually see God restore this world back to Himself.

Ray Edwards explains the origins of the concept of the 7-Mountains saying that *"In 1975, Bill Bright (the founder of Campus Crusade) was having lunch in Colorado with Loren Cunningham (who founded Youth with a Mission).*

Both men had been given a dream by God, containing a message to give to the other. That message was about Seven Mountains of influence. Francis Schaeffer received a similar message from the Lord at about the same time. All three believed that in order for the Church to impact the world for Jesus Christ, it would be necessary for us to influence the Seven Mountains of society." (4)

The mountains became defined by them as:

1.   Media, Arts and Entertainment
2.   Business
3.   Education
4.   Family
5.   Government
6.   Medical
7.   Religion

Now, as this is not a particularly theological or Biblical explanation of the world, you are more than welcome to find more mountains of influence, or sub-divide various areas down. It's just a way of expressing how modern society has developed around significant centres of authority, so don't be overly distracted by it.

I find it useful and I believe, as a Kingdom people of "Salt and Light", you and I will have a calling to transform one or more of these seven mountains, or at least some small part of one. Together, we can make a disproportionate difference to the world! I always like to think that your pulse will probably race a little as you hear about the sphere you were made to reach and so I'm going to give you a chance to discover that right now. Are you ready?

In "500" I prophesied over the 7 spheres, words that I felt God give me for the new era that we are now entering. Prophetically imagine with me the Kingdom of God coming to these spheres as I paint a picture of God's heart for our world:

The Mountain Of Politics & Government

In 2017 God said to me:

My glory will invade politics, carried on the shoulders of the ambassadors of heaven. Men and women who have met me in my glory, will be given the opportunity and mantle to stand for office and call my presence in.

Prayer meetings will run like rivers through parliament buildings. The EU will become engulfed in a war for its soul, as the Kingdom of light begins to penetrate even the darkest corners.

The war for power in the boardrooms and cabinet rooms of the world will rage, but a new grace from my hand, that seems to melt even the greatest authorities will begin to invade meetings and conversations. While some have felt an "Elijah-like" confrontation will be the thing that transforms people of power, it will actually be a release of softening grace that will melt the hearts of kings and presidents. This is the age of grace and glory. Favour from the hand of God and man will be released in the earth, and the Church will be established as prince among the mountains.

A rising of a new type of missionary from the Church will begin to transform politics locally – strong, spiritual, biblically literate and fearless, the Church will march into the political arena ready to be a city on a hill.

The Mountain Of Media & The Arts

Over the arts God said to me:

The Church will become known again as a womb of creativity – art, music, words, media - Christian artists will be recognised as the source of immense creative expertise – as training schools in the arts arise in every city, nation and continent.

Film makers will send shockwaves throughout the world, explaining the fallen brokenness of man, melting the hardness of pride and releasing a longing for divine grace and healing. It is the arts, not politics, that will touch and reshape the morality of nations back to the image of God. Through stories, song, the retelling of divine history, the arts will capture the hearts of humanity and make many question the moral anarchy that has swept the world.

Stadiums will be used for church services again and again. The greatest auditoriums in the land will be filled. Arts and signs and wonders will run like streams, blending into a river of grace and glory that will capture the hearts of millions. Kings, presidents, the influencers of the world will weep in worship at the presence of God. Royalty will fall prostrate before the Father's presence.

Revivals will accompany theatre companies. Anointed productions will be performed that lead the audience to overwhelming travailing of soul. Queues will go on endlessly as people long to be in God's presence and hear the words once again. Audience members will convulse in their seats, cry out, rush the stage, run out to the streets, overcome by the Holy Spirit's presence, in deep repentance. Some will be left overnight in the theatre, as the glory of God moves and crowds become immobile under the hand of God's glory. In some areas this will become considered a normal response to the arts, such is the power and anointing of God at work.

Successful and renowned singers will begin to turn their concerts into evangelistic campaigns – even giving away bibles, taking altar calls and working with local churches. In some great auditoriums, multiple celebrities will give testimony and perform, with thousands giving their lives to Christ and leaving new churches planted.

Small radio stations will spring up across the earth broadcasting the Gospel, power and presence of God – telling the stories, releasing the testimonies of communities in regional areas. They will become the new pulpits of the airwaves. Thousands will be healed simply by listening, as the wisdom and wonder of God floods the airwaves. Some of these places will become so successful, larger stations will model themselves on the pattern of these glory stations.

The Arts have long been a bone of contention to the Church, as immorality, immaturity and unsanctified behaviour can run rife. But this is an area we must learn to negotiate boldly if we are to reach this area of influence.

Glory Invading Education

Over education God showed me:

Schools, colleges and universities will be in upheaval at the moves of revival. Christian unions will hold prayer meetings that fill up like assemblies. Outpourings of the Spirit will interrupt classes. Teachers will at times become preachers, as God's presence moves so strongly in the classrooms. Many will fall to the floor overcome by God's presence.

Great wars will be fought around the classrooms, as the enemy vies for the minds of the young – but the glory of God will prevail. Schools, colleges and universities will be swept up in visitations of glory so strong, that head teachers will be unable to finish prayers and speeches, and as they weep under the hand of God and the young people assembled begin to sing under the infilling of the Spirit.

"Missionary" will become a common recommendation for careers advice – the hunger for millions to carry God's glory to the ends of the earth will grow, as the compulsion of love drives a new generation to invade every last corner of the earth with the Gospel.

God & Medicine

Speaking of the mountain of medicine I felt God say:

God's glory will empty some hospitals. Saints will go in, and prayer will fast become another normalised route to wellness. There will be many times when wards are emptied by the visit of a group of glory carriers.

But what is more remarkable is that it will become acceptable again for doctors to pray and lay hands on the sick. They will see the dead raised, intensive care patients radically healed, and many will come to faith in hospital.

In many places, prayer will become actively recognized, taught and recommended as a legitimate means of healing. Some medical universities will specialise in prayer for healing, helping to release an army of "divine doctors" able to walk in miracles and medicine.

Some hospitals will develop "miracle teams" who are trained and released to move around the hospitals praying, caring and comforting the sick. Churches will be set up in hospital wings.
As I write today, I also feel God saying that a new type of medical innovator is being released in these days, bringing a flood of new strategies, blueprints, ideas and solutions to this field.
As my friend Drew Neal would say "Let the Solutionaries arise!"

God & The Family

Over the Family God would say:

The make up of the family will be restored not by the laws of man, but by a movement of grace upon the broken hearts of humanity. The oil of God's grace will flow upon the earth, and through encounter after encounter, the hearts of humanity, so hungry for approval and acceptance, will be restored to the Father's Heart.

There will be outpost, after outpost, where a restoration of families will become the norm; divorce will drastically reduce, fatherlessness will fade, sexual confusion will give way to peace and holiness. In some places it will be the Church that become the "father and mother" of communities, bringing stability, nourishment, approval, discipline and tenderness. The Church will seem, in some places, to be almost a parental figure in a nation, rather than an irrelevant relic. Adoption and fostering ministries will explode across church communities, as God sets the lonely in healthy families.

God's Glory On Businesses & Financial Institutions

In speaking of business and finance I felt God say:

Businessmen will be touched powerfully by glory and become Generals of Commerce – releasing finances and resources into the global harvest. But not only will they resource ministries and churches, but their very businesses will become strongholds of the Kingdom, bringing societal transformation and change. Godly businessmen and women will be seen as spiritual elders in the cities, and many will run churches alongside, and even within, their businesses and among their staff. The commitment to transform a city or region will mean businesses become places of Kingdom rulership, to better advance the glory of God across and area.

The glory of God will disrupt the business day again and again! It will seem some leaders will have to trust that everything will get done, and profits will be made, as some will give up days to prayer and seeking God, allowing staff to be in God's presence, rather than remaining on "the production line." But these businesses will prosper greatly in God's hand – bringing wealth and influence for the Kingdom.

The Knowledge Of His Glory Filling The Earth

If we return to the simplicity of encountering God in the place of prayer, and then faithfully run to the mountains of Kingdom mission wherever He sends, I have no doubt it will lead to the glory of the Lord being known globally as never before!

Habakkuk 2:14 clearly states that *"The knowledge of the glory of the Lord is going to cover the earth as the waters cover the sea."* Slowly, God's glory will invade the whole earth, until she is saturated by the growing waves of His grace.

Let me prophesy – *"God's presence will seem to hover over entire cities. An unusual atmosphere, sometimes of sombre conviction, and at other times of great joy, will seem to pervade the streets and businesses.*

Mass evangelism, something some have thought was a thing of the past, will become widespread, as crowds fill auditoriums, stadiums, arenas, fields and city centres. Worship will go on for hours, many thousands will be overcome by the strong presence of God, miracles and manifestations of the Spirit will take place – sometimes "performed" by believers, at other times, simply by the hand of God on a city."

Do you, like me, want to get away from fruitless busyness of dull religion and return to the adventure of meeting Him, hearing Him and taking the Kingdom wherever He sends us? Then take the time to carve out of your life the things that steal from that time, focus and energy, and get back to the presence of the King – do it quickly, there is much for us to do!

Sources

1a.https://simple.wikipedia.org/wiki/Ecclesia_(Church)#:~:text=Latin%20ecclesia%2C%20 from%20Greek%20ekklesia,%22%2C%20or%20%22convocation%22.

1. https://www.youtube.com/watch?v=I-VPGDWQuDg

2. https://en.wikipedia.org/wiki/Elvis_Presley#1973%E2%80%931977:_Health_deterioration_and_ death

3. http://www.reallifestories.org/stories/elvis-presley/

4. https://rayedwards.com/the-seven-mountains/

JOURNAL & SESSION 5
DISCUSSION TIME

Use the questions below to ponder and journal, or to discuss this chapter with your small group or team.

1. Can you clearly define the difference between the Church and the Kingdom?

2. Why is it important to let the "weeds and wheat" grow together? How could you better fulfil this mandate, without compromising your holy standards as a church?

3. Why is internal church discipline still necessary, even though the Kingdom must express great grace to the world? Do you conduct discipline correctly, as a church?

4. Do you have any of your own stories of the *"disproportionate"* effect of bringing Kingdom influence on a situation? Do you have any of your own stories of the *"birds of the air"* wanting to *rest in the Kingdom branches* of your community? Discuss them.

5. The 7 mountains that the Kingdom must influence are 1) Media, Arts & Entertainment 2) Business 3) Education 4) Family 5) Government 6) Medical 7) Religion. Of these seven, which do you personally, and corporately, feel you must impact?

6. Another way to discern this is to ask, which of the 7 mountain prophecies that make up the second half of this chapter, most stirred and excited you?

7. How could you develop a powerful strategy to impact the mountains of influence God has given you?

JOURNAL

JOURNAL

10 The Lord says...

"This stirring that is growing in your heart, even now, will lead to a journey of personal reinvention and divine innovation, resulting in a transformation of the very behaviours, methods and even the beliefs of many Christians. While the essentials of my Gospel remain untouched, rather than live safely within the doctrinal walls of your favoured denomination, I am calling you out to a brave new era through the unveiling of new ideas, new graces and new perspectives in ministry. Some will call it a new Age of Innovation in the Church. Adventure, explore, run in the sheer joy of my counsel my people, for I am about to perform a wonder in the earth that will usher many into the Kingdom!"

Chapter 10
A New Era Of Kingdom Innovation

"You can't solve a problem on the same level that it was creat-
ed. You have to rise above it to the next level."
– Albert Einstein

For several years I have been prophesying the release of a new wave of innovation in the Church. I believed new ideas, methods, styles, systems and strategies were about to flood the Church, lifting her and empowering her Kingdom mandate like never before.

Well, hasn't God enforced a release of innovation in 2020? The global pandemic has struck at the mundanity of our methods, and we have been pivoted into a season of deep innovative thinking, along with a very steep learning curve!

On 13 April 2020 God showed me a vision of the iron structures that began to flourish because of the Industrial Revolution. I believe, in similar fashion, this genesis of a new era will be a tipping point where tools, methods and collaborations we had never previously imagined, would become natural, and there would be a flourishing of new ways, approaches and tactics because of these new tools and materials available.

One obvious way this has instantly impacted the Church recently is the need to become digital and online in our connection, as for some it has been the only way to minister through the lockdowns of 2020. People who have hated social media have now embraced the usefulness of being able to connect down a phone, a computer or TV screen. Churches are very aware of, if not awash with, fresh interest from millions who are now dipping their toes into the ocean of opportunities the Church provides. The world of the internet and social media is a mission-field the Church simply cannot ignore, as literally billions sit poised and longing for impact. They are connected yet often lonely, just the other side of a screen – if we will just go!

Before the pandemic I had a dream. In it God had given me innovative new ways to help people online in their homes. I wasn't particularly keen on the idea if I'm honest, as I prefer meeting people "in-person", but I'm so glad I obeyed the heavenly vision, and my wife and I converted our garage into a studio for a new form of online learning community. The Tribe is now enjoying friendship and ministering to growing hundreds of people across the globe, with our membership exploding during the lockdowns of 2020!

To add to the basic idea of helping people online through the Tribe, my wife Victoria developed a whole new learning system, supported by software used by the likes of Harvard University, and now our Tribe members enjoy learning from the many modules on leadership, the prophetic, revival and theology we offer online.

Next Vicky stretched to become an app maker, delivering content through people's smartphones. For each of these successful innovations, she would simply get an idea from God, enlist in what we fondly call *The University of YouTube* (i.e. "Just let me go find a video that'll teach me how to do that!") and off she goes, innovating, exploring and experimenting in new ways to see God's Kingdom come and lives discipled!

Innovations In Your Soul

But innovating isn't only about the tools and methods we use, but it's also about who we are and what we are becoming ourselves.

My wife Vicky is a very capable, loyal and godly woman, but has very little desire to be seen; indeed she would always shun the stage whenever possible.

But as 2020 began to unfold she felt God nudging her to start delivering daily devotional broadcasts through social media, something she would never have imagined doing! As she has pushed herself in little more than raw obedience to God's voice, you can see a fresh new innovative chapter is unfolding into the new purposes of God within her.

At first, new ideas from God usually start as faltering steps, perhaps a little fearful, unsure that it is even God speaking. But slowly the exploring turns to established concepts, the concepts turn to innovations and eventually the innovations become influence. Before you know it, you're on a whole new adventure with God, His favour smiling on your soul, your confidence growing and your horizons broadening before you!

We must put our souls in the place where we can hear God breathe fresh ideas into our hearts. We must never fear failure. We must learn how to learn again and redeem the awkward nervousness of it all. After all, as one of my favourite preachers Rick Godwin says *"You'll never get better if you keep chasing EASY!"*

Digital Revolution In The Church

As I've already said, the most obvious innovation for the Church in this time has been the discovery of a whole new mission field in the world of social media. For me, this began some years before…

It was Easter 1997. I was sitting in my rented apartment, having spent all week at the revival in Pensacola, USA. The week of meetings was over, but I had that 'God-sense' that something more was still to take place.

I lay on the sofa, surfing the channels of U.S. TV, my feet up on the arm rest and my head propped up by a stack of pillows. Eventually I flicked on to a Christian channel where a pastor was being interviewed. Something inside me said "Watch, I'm going to talk to you".

I sat listening to the live interview when suddenly the pastor turned to the camera, interrupted his flow and said *"and you young man, laying on the sofa in that apartment, with your feet up on the end of the sofa and those pillows behind your head.*

Listen up; God's going to speak to you!"

I screamed! Images of TV prank shows flashed through my mind! Half of me was filled with the fear of God, the other half wanted to look for the hidden cameras!

I sat transfixed for some minutes and eventually a young woman was interviewed. Halfway through her interview she began to prophecy, and God spoke to me so powerfully that I will never forget it. In fact, I am living today in the good of that God-happening.

The word she gave had been about my role in my local church, but another powerful lesson was also learned that day – the opportunity for God to speak had been afforded to me through a screen. From that day on I knew that media could be an incredible way to reach into homes and touch lives with God's power.

Now in the UK our image of Christian broadcasting is often overshadowed by an American history of adulterous TV hosts, manipulative money raising tactics and hype-filled emotionalism. But an old hero of mine once said *"The answer to mis-use is not non-use; but correct use"*.

I am convinced that social media could be so powerful if Christians were willing to take their stand and use the incredible opportunities that are coming about today as a result of our learning new ways throughout this pandemic period.

Here are two great reasons why churches should not ignore this time to stretch out into media ministry:

Social Media Goes Where You Cannot

In these days when door knocking J.W.'s and salesmen are pretty well loathed, TV, radio and social media can beam straight into every house or car, to every phone and computer and minister God's love and truth to a suspicious world.

I recently received the following email: *"I became a Born-Again Christian after listening to you on the radio. I just want to say*

I have been listening to your programmes every morning on radio and I think they are really great, really inspiring and they help me to start the day … our youngest daughter is also now saved."

Isn't this what it's all about? Just last Sunday a lady turned up at our church from Leeds. She had been listening to our programming on radio, got saved, and just had to turn up to tell us! Your voice can go places your body can't go! It can reach out to those in homes, hospitals and cars with the Gospel and provide answers to life's pain.

New Media Is Affordable

Never has media ministry been so affordable. The fast pace of technology means prices are continually driven down, and with wise decisions, a church or ministry can set up a social media, television or radio programme to touch potential millions, for a relatively small budget. Last week I was interviewed by one radio show that reaches billions! All you need is a smart phone, a social media account and you can start.

It is so satisfying for me to know that every sermon I prepare and preach will not only touch a few hundred lives in our church building, but will also be recorded, edited and broadcast on the internet. We have listeners from as far afield as Japan and Australia, and from as unlikely places as the prisons of Britain to newly reached tribal areas of foreign lands. I have even heard of missionaries on the Honduran Bay Islands, who gather all their friends in their home to join us for church services. All this for a minuscule budget by comparative standards.

The fast pace of technology development means it is going to be ever easier for churches to embrace the social media age. Today, well over 50% of people would rather watch TV on the internet, which I believe will lead to radical development of TV stations on-line, for a fraction of the cost of traditional broadcasting.

Don't be tempted to back off your online presence in the coming years. We should go online, unless God specifically says otherwise, as it opens the doors for a continual flow of seekers looking for God. You'd welcome them gladly to your building, so why not welcome them to your broadcast too?

Rethinking Church In Other Ways

Of course, the move to online outreach, community and discipleship has been an obvious shift for many churches, but other innovations are also breaking out with many more to come that I simply cannot imagine as I write, I'm sure of it! But my friend Dan McCollam says *"Imagination is the most powerful nation on earth"* and I do see some people brilliantly exploring new imaginative territory as we enter this new era.

I know of new types of relationship and collaborations with organisations nearby and far afield, as online connection removes geographical boundaries. There are new online training schools emerging, business ventures that are creating bridges into communities, evangelistic tools (The famed Alpha Course has THRIVED online during the Pandemic, with some churches starting courses daily!). Off-line, fresh political roles are evolving, new global networks opening up, some work places might soon feel more like church spaces, and new church models are arising that don't look anything like church as we've known it!

Many leaders are radically rethinking church itself. Some that have busied themselves with an over emphasis on Sunday services, to the point where the focus on prayer and mission has been lost, are even considering meeting only once a month for a traditional Sunday service, in order to give more time to deeper encounters in the place of prayer, and greater influence in the realms of Kingdom come. Some are feeling they simply have to find ways to give greater emphasis to mission and community engagement.

Some are dropping Sunday services in favour of other time slots to meet in order to reach specific new communities. You are never going to reach a clubbing young society with your 9am Sunday service... time to rethink our time slots!

Others are considering venturing into new types of multi-site church. Perhaps not the mega church model of the U.S. but rather a missional creative model that fits unique local demographics and geography. If this interests you, grab my book *"The Multi-site Church Adventure"* (1) for inspiration. We have been exploring this for a few years!

Some are considering micro-churches in homes, broadcast services to home groups, and even "Watch Party" churches inspired by the Facebook tool, allowing groups to join a service together, online.

Others are investigating entirely new forms of "internet Church membership" where people can become church members from across a vast geographical area, sometimes in addition to an existing membership of a church where they live, or even instead of, due to their remote location.

Some of these internet-based believers are in quiet evangelical churches, and deeply respect and love the sense of family found there, but equally desire a more Spirit-filled experience, and so are twinning an online membership to a distant Spirit-filled church, alongside their local church affiliation.

Churches open to innovation for Kingdom purposes will begin to accommodate this more and more, and see it as a way for us to be further "One" in Him, without any sense of competition. We are going to find churches that allow access to resources and connection, without demanding classic membership increasingly arise. There will be people who seem to belong to several churches, with completely blurred lines of membership, but that are far from the "spiritual gypsy" that church leaders used to fear.

Perhaps we are finally becoming one team, one Church, working together like never before? Will it be abused and go wrong at times? Of course! It always has. But for many, the tidal wave of innovation about to crash upon the Church will require a radical rethink of some of our baseless fears, our long-held practices, or even our theology.

To some this new, innovative unity will be as radical as the Reformation. Which is partly why the next chapter is titled as it is.

Sources
1.https://www.amazon.co.uk/Multi-Site-Church-Adventure-Jarrod-Cooper-ebook/dp/B07VH-PVN44

JOURNAL & SESSION 6 DISCUSSION TIME

Use the questions below to ponder and journal, or to discuss this chapter with your small group or team.

1. How has your church been innovative lately?

2. Unless you feel particularly instructed by God *not* to, how can you better use social media and online broadcasting to further your mission?

3. Using a flip chart, list all your church activities. Note the activities where people have been newly saved in the last 12 months with a *. How could you make other activities more like the ones that successfully see people born again?

4. What activities are no longer fruitful and need to stop?

5. What things do you do that are simply cultural, and not biblical? What other ways could you do these things, to bring a fresh innovative energy to them?

6. If you knew that Jesus was returning in 3 months, what would you do to reach your region? Why not let some of the innovative and energetic ideas from that discussion infiltrate your plans for the future?

7. What are you going to do to make your culture more innovative?

JOURNAL

JOURNAL

FROM UNITY TO COLLABORATION

11 The Lord says...

"The prideful pretence of unity among my people grieves my heart, and so I am about to release a fresh grace in you for new collaborative endeavours. You will be over-joyed with the work of grace in your heart that begins to find pure, selfless pleasure in the family of my people. Rather than conducting mere unity events, I will empower you to walk in a new spirit of collaboration, partnership and alliance. I am also forming great new apostolic tribes of brothers and sisters in this day, all joined in love, filled with joy, kissed with my favour. Many of the old organisational structures of your youth will be deconstructed and crumble at the weight and speed of the innovations, pace and glory about to be released. Look for true fellowship, for there you will find my favour."

Chapter 11
From Unity To Collaboration

"Finding good players is easy. Getting them to play as a team is another story." - Casey Stengel

I love the Margaret Mead quote *"Never doubt that a small group of thoughtful, committed people can change the world. Indeed. It is the only thing that ever has."*

For about a year the Lord has called out to my spirit that the Church is about to move beyond mere event-based unity, to a place of deeper, selfless collaboration.

"How good and pleasant it is
    when God's people live together in unity!
It is like precious oil poured on the head,
    running down on the beard,
running down on Aaron's beard,
    down on the collar of his robe.
It is as if the dew of Hermon
    were falling on Mount Zion.
For there the LORD bestows his blessing,
    even life forevermore." Psalm 133:1-3

Unity is good of course. Many of us can remember the old unity events right back to the 1980's. But our first attempts at unity in those days seemed to be about singing together in a building, ensuring we give equal platform time to each minister, dodging around doctrinal or positional insecurities and prayer meetings that always lowered themselves stylistically to the least offensive rung of the ladder. It was a start, it was good, but it wasn't full unity. We still need to journey quite some way beyond those days.

One church leader laughed as he recounted his experience of

the 1980's unity events to me - *"We had a unity event called 'Together for the Kingdom' - but we weren't together and it wasn't very Kingdom. We all argued about the cassette tape sales afterward!"*

The drive for unity has continued to develop since those early 80's efforts, and there are now many unity meetings I could be in each month. As a minister I could literally spend most days in some networking meeting or another (and some do!). But surely unity, true unity, is about more than whether we pray together or turn up at each other's gatherings?

Unity Is Not...

Let me attempt to describe unity, by describing what unity is *not*. I'm going to be a bit cheeky again here, and grossly over stereotype, but let me have some fun for a moment. In my 30 years of church leadership, I have discovered that unity is not...

Unity is not a group of leaders sat in a room together (just because they are together it certainly does not mean they are *united!*).

Unity is not a gathering of saints from across a region, singing songs, and desperately keeping the meeting to the lowest common denominator, so as not to offend. Gatherings should reflect & celebrate our strengths, not run from them.

Unity is not a committee. Biblical unity is led by God-ordained 5-fold ministry (Ephesians 4:11-16), not managerial organising committees.

Unity is not formed by making leaders feel guilty and leprous if someone doesn't turn up to your network meeting. Leaders are busy, often over-worked. I always make sure leaders invited to our events know that I understand they cannot make every meeting, everywhere, all the time. Let's support each other, not drain each other!

Unity is not an event at all! Unity is brothers *"dwelling together"* and living together as Psalm 133 tells us. All the events in the world won't cure the unloving, unfriendly heart. If we don't love, we need to repent, not attend another meeting!

Unity is not a cure-all. The Bible indeed says that *"one will chase a thousand, two 10,000"* (Deuteronomy 32:20), but that doesn't mean that one weakling can team up with another weakling and suddenly *"Hey Presto!"* they're powerful in God! It is actually talking about one who can already chase 1,000, teaming up with another awesome, God-filled person. When humble heroes team up with other heroes, amazing things happen. When plebs team up, you just get two plebs!

Unity is not me giving up my belief in the miraculous to keep others happy. I can no more edit the miraculous out of my life, than I can edit it from scripture. And a Bible devoid of the miraculous is a very small book, with maps.

Unity is not possible if you feel threatened. Love cannot exist where leaders are competitive, jealous, envious, self-centred or carrying agendas for power. Unity can only exist where we humbly serve each other fearlessly.

Unity is not *the* answer, Jesus is! Nor is it always good. God had to destroy the unity of Babel (Genesis 11) as they were united for all the wrong reasons. *"A friend of fools suffers harm"* says Proverbs 13:20 indicating that you need to choose carefully where you bond. The prophet Jeremiah said *"I sat alone because your hand was upon me"* (Jeremiah 15:17) teaching us there are times when solitude is heavens prescription for godliness.

And so I hope you can see, I believe unity in the form of events or falsely constructed organisational relationships are not some easy cure that will bring revival. Rather, we simply need to repent of our unloving, envious hearts, be friends, act as brothers and start getting the Kingdom job done collaboratively!

Love Is…

OK, I know I'm being a tad provocative. Let me lighten the mood by talking about what true unity actually is….

"Make every effort to keep the unity of the Spirit through the bond of peace." Ephesians 4:3

Unity is a spirit, an attitude, a love among us, not an organisation. It is how we think, act and feel about each other, being generous to each other, genuinely seeking each other's best. Unity is laughter, peace, friendship, fun, understanding, sacrificial generosity, forgiveness, patience & thoughtfulness.

It is when I'm still cheering you on, whether you irritate, inspire, fall behind or race ahead of me. It is basic Christian behaviour, outworked among churches, ministers and disciples. Events are never going to cut it. We want the SPIRIT of unity flowing among us.

But now let me go a step further. I actually do believe many places I visit are beginning to truly grasp the above reality of unity, as leaders begin to deeply care for each other and cheer each other on, rather than seeing other church leaders as "the competition." I am even told by my U.S. friends that the United Kingdom is something of a global forerunner in this spirit of unity, which is wonderful to hear!

Time For Collaboration

But I do believe in this coming season we are going to grow up from mere unity events, and good friendships (both good in their own way, despite what I've provocatively said so far!) to a place of *real collaboration*. God is going to join churches together, and churches with businesses and churches with local councils. He'll bond itinerant ministries with local fellowships in a way that has never happened before. Para-Church and Church are coming together! Local churches will share buildings, resources, leaders, staff and even members (Get your head around that one!). No church will care who gets the praise, has the most platform time, got the most new converts, or ended up paying the most!

The coming move of unity and collaboration is going to deeply challenge the pride, envy, the spirit of competition and the spirit of religion within us. It will start a fierce war in the hearts of some! But we're also going to start to experience the most humble, sweet, selfless expressions of the Kingdom roll out across the earth as the Body of Christ starts to walk in unpretentious power, deep love and gracious mercy, like never before. Self-promoting, brand addicted, ego-centric preachers will be swept aside by modest, self-effacing, Jesus-magnifying servant leaders. What a glorious bride the Church will be!

It's in this time that God is going to orchestrate the joining of unassuming, loving and powerful leaders to work together to expand the Kingdom in a given geographical area or sphere. We're going to feel like bands of brothers taking on the enemy, living generously, loving outrageously! But be warned, it will only come to those who let the fire of God burn their envious, jealous, insecure hearts with His holiness.

As we enter the new era, be brave and ask yourself fiery, tough questions like these:

- What attitudes in me are hindering true unity?
- Am I insecure and how does it affect my relationships?
- Am I jealous and envious of other leaders?
- Does my envy cause me to speak harshly of other leaders, either in private or to them personally?
- Am I as kind as I should be?
- Do I truly behave as if the Church in my area is one unified team?
- Am I wasting my time with unity events that aren't true unity? How could they become places of true unity?
- Who should I collaborate with?
- What would Jesus do with the Church in my region if He had His way fully?

Helen Keller said *"Alone we can do so little; together we can do so much."* Ryunosuke Satoro stated *"Individually, we are one drop. Together, we are an ocean."* Jesus said *"By this everyone will know that you are my disciples, if you love one another."* (John 13:35) This is perhaps one of the greatest challenges to us today, but it could also lead to the greatest glory.

Jesus said these amazing words as He prayed for you and I.

Let us do all we can to ensure this prayer is answered in our lifetime:

"I pray also for those who will believe in me through their message, that all of them may be one, Father, just as you are in me and I am in you. May they also be in us so that the world may believe that you have sent me. I have given them the glory that you gave me, that they may be one as we are one— I in them and you in me—so that they may be brought to complete unity. Then the world will know that you sent me and have loved them even as you have loved me." John 17:20-23

JOURNAL & SESSION 7 DISCUSSION TIME

Use the questions below to ponder and journal, or to discuss this chapter with your small group or team.

1. As a general opening discussion, chat about these questions from the chapter:
    *   What attitudes in me are hindering true unity?
    *   Am I insecure and how does it affect my relationships?
    *   Am I jealous and envious of other leaders?
    *   Does my envy cause me to speak harshly of other leaders, either in private or to them personally?
    *   Am I as kind as I should be?
    *   Do I truly behave as if the Church in my area is one unified team?
    *   Am I wasting my time with unity events that aren't true unity? How could they become places of true unity?
    *   Who should I collaborate with?
    *   What would Jesus do with the Church in my region if He had His way fully?

2. Do you need to forgive anyone as a Church team, for splits, dis-unity, gossip or hatred. How might you address that?

3. Where could your church community collaborate deeply with other churches/ministries nearby?

4. What hinders our unity and collaborations?

5. Discuss this statement: *Love and unity should be universal, but **collaboration** usually requires a divine call to work closely together. It should not be forced.*

6. How could you foster unity more in the churches of your area?

7. What is the wildest, most loving and selfless thing you could do for churches near you? Make a plan to do something that will grow the unity in your area.

JOURNAL

JOURNAL

12 The Lord says...

"I am releasing the "spirit of Elijah" upon the earth once again (Matthew 17:11-13). The hearts of the fathers and the children will be brought to a place of sweet unity (Malachi 4:5-6). I am no longer content to move only in the middle ground - I am moving to the edges and releasing a glory over the little children and an empowering upon an older generation. This will be a sign in the earth: "Little ones will lead them" (Isaiah 11:6) while your "old men will dream dreams" (Acts 2:17) and their hearts will "throb and swell with joy!" (Isaiah 60:5). Look out for the rise of the Fathers and Mothers in the Church like never before. A new mission mandate is being placed before the older generation, who will embrace the call to mission even in their final years on earth – a generation is arising that will seek me for "refirement more than retirement!"

Chapter 12
Silver Surfers & Divine Arrows

"One father is more than a hundred schoolmasters."
– George Herbert

In Luke's Gospel we're clearly shown that John the Baptist came in the spirit of Elijah, with an incredible message to prepare the world for Christ's ministry. Speaking of John, Luke's Gospel says:

"He will also go before Him in the spirit and power of Elijah, 'to turn the hearts of the fathers to the children,' ... to make ready a people prepared for the Lord." Luke 1:13-17

Here Luke is connecting John's ministry with a prophecy in Malachi, about someone coming in the power of Elijah, just before the Messiah appears. It tells of a divine unction being released through that person, which will produce inter-generational unity and co-operation:

"See, I will send the prophet Elijah to you before that great and dreadful day of the LORD comes. He will turn the hearts of the parents to their children, and the hearts of the children to their parents." Malachi 4:5-6

Intergenerational unity, according to Malachi, Luke, John the Baptist and even Jesus Himself, is one of the main preparation grounds for any move of God. When soft-hearted fathers and mothers (both natural and spiritual), turn to the young, insecure and inexperienced around them, and start to teach, comfort and cheer them on, the environment is primed for God to move.

As the elder generation turns in love towards the younger, the generations align together, unity forms, and a Kingdom atmosphere emerges. The Passion of youth becomes harnessed and established by the wisdom of years. The tiredness in some who have travelled far and long, gives way to the fresh passion in the idealistic eyes of the young. Wisdom meets energy. Stability undergirds passion. Experience is reignited by idealism. This is where the Kingdom thrives!

I encountered such a culture a while ago, when a friend's youth-filled church became a beautiful home for a man in his 80's.

"How do you cope with the loud music?" the old man was asked, as it was obvious his longings for gentle hymns were never going to be met in an environment of pumping rhythms, lights and smoke machines.

"Oh, that's easy!" was his response, "I just take my hearing aid out!"

That is a *turned* Kingdom heart. Being a father to an orphaned and confused world included comprehending that music styles were mere cultural gift-wrapping, not the essence of things. It was the opportunity to be a father and support to hundreds of youngsters that truly mattered eternally.

The Silver Surfers Arise

I see two generational course corrections emerging as we enter the new era. It is as if the *Spirit of Elijah* is at work again in this Divine Reset time – In my own words, I'd say the *Silver Surfers are Rising*, and the *Young Arrows are being Released*.

In recent years, in many successful and well celebrated churches around the world, it would be easy to conclude that God was only passionate about promoting the young, profiling the beautiful and using the trendy! Ha! Of course, deep down we know that's not true, and I'm sure most of us are simply so pleased to see any church packed the rafters with young people.

However, the subtle downside of high-profile churches being led by trendy, young, skinny-jean-wearing hipsters, is that it can seem anyone sprouting a little too much grey hair should soon consider retirement! Being in the ministry can sometimes seem like the plight of the female actress in Hollywood, as meaningful roles get "harder to land" the older you get! But is there really such a thing as being "past it" when it comes to your calling from God?

Well, as someone who has purposefully tried to push down the age range of our leadership teams and platform in order to appeal to younger seekers, I have also noticed God is clearly speaking into a whole new adventure for the older saint, what I might call the grey-haired "Silver Surfer" as we enter this new era!

Recently Bill Yount, a prophetic author and advisor at large for Aglow International, shared this prophetic word to the older generation:

"I hear the Father saying, "I am breaking the age barrier! Quit saying, 'I am getting older.' Christ in you is ageless. Allow His Spirit to quicken your mortal body and soar with the eagles. And don't tell Me where I can't send you this year. Get over yourself and buy some new luggage." (Someone should be shouting about now!)

I sense the Lord saying, "The older stars in My kingdom are going to shine brighter and do greater exploits than ever before!" I sense there is a special anointing coming upon older men and women in the Body of Christ. God is not through using you. Your age is not against you, it is for you. Job 12:12 says, "Wisdom is with the elderly, and understanding comes with long life." You have more wisdom now than ever. With years comes understanding.

This anointing is going to cause you to live longer. Many of you have not planned to live long enough. It will be an anointing similar to Caleb when he reached 85 years. He said to the Lord, "I am as strong now as when I was forty, and I want to take another mountain!" There is coming a "spiritual fountain of youth" into your midst, a renewing, a release of God's strength. Psalm 68:28 says, "Your God has commanded your strength." God is commanding His strength into you! One translation says, "Your God has decided you will be strong!"

Many of you are going to have to live longer because God is not through using you. Many of you are going to go into a second "childhood" in the Spirit. You will be reactivated by God to live out your dreams that you are just dreaming about right now. People and relatives will laugh and say, "You are going to do what? You are going to go where? At your age?" But that anointing is going to rise up within you to take mountains, to do exploits, to run and not be weary, to walk and not faint (see Isa. 40:31).

Our older years are when we are in our prime to be used and bring forth fruit. Psalm 91:16 says, "With long life I will satisfy you and show you My salvation." There is an anointing coming upon God's people to live longer. The joy of the Lord which is our strength is lengthening our days upon the earth.

Many have made out their wills, but before you think about leaving, check out your Father's will for you. I don't think you are going anywhere for a while. As Abraham and Sarah conceived in old age, you are about to conceive and live to see your Isaac—your impossible dream!

Remember, "too old" is not in the Bible."[1]

I love that! Prepare to live longer!

The Rise Of The Fathers

Like Caleb, still hungry to pioneer "one more mountain" in his old age (Joshua 14:6-15), I believe God is given a second wind to the purposes and dreams of what I call the Silver Surfers. As some reach retirement age, God is going to give you *refirement* instead!

There is a new rising of the fathers emerging in the Church right now (I mean that in a gender-neutral way...so, mothers too!). New missionary ventures, business endeavours, apostolic responsibility, powerful advisory positions and much more await the grey-haired fathers and mothers of the Lord in the Church. We need to make sure we are recognising, utilising and releasing an entire generation of spiritual parents that are far from the end of their lives at 65, now the expected age to live healthy and strong is far exceeding that.

I believe there are some who will spend their final years on earth launching into new mission ventures, offering their silver-haired years as a sacrifice to reach one more land, save one more city, touch one more culture and take one more mountain for the Kingdom.

To add to that, this generation have a responsibility to help father and even *"grand-parent"* a young generation coming through. The danger of a gaping chasm between Church generations, is that entire age-groups might learn nothing of historic revivals, we may lose centuries worth of deep theology, and find one day that our prayer rooms are empty and our activities powerless. Some youngsters might be more easily drawn by form, than substance and it is a parent's role to draw the young into the deep end of God's workings. A young generation may easily know all the paraphernalia of Church, but never know God's glory, or how to host or revere His power among us. Fathers must show us the way.

"My father didn't tell me how to live. He lived and let me watch him do it," said Clarence Budington Kelland. This is why the Silver Surfers must turn to the young "Arrows of the Lord" and help stabilise them, ready for the coming moves of God as we enter this new era. The Father wants us to start working together!

Frederick Douglass said *"It is easier to build strong children than to repair broken men."* Walter M. Schirra, Sr. stated *"You don't raise heroes, you raise sons. And if you treat them like sons, they'll turn out to be heroes, even if it's just in your own eyes."*

Silver Surfer, can you imagine the sheer joy of passing on your knowledge to fresh faced, wide-eyed generation of idealistic youngsters, and seeing them travel far and wide in the things of God? All you have to do is start treating them like sons, letting your heart be moved and turned towards them, and the ground will be prepared for a fresh move of God.

The Young Arrows Of God

"Like arrows in the hands of a warrior are children born in one's youth." Psalm 127:4

Here the Psalmist speaks of children as weapons, specifically arrows. The images to learn from here are many:

They are meant to be in our hands, close to us. At hand.

We are meant to polish, cherish and prepare them to be launched with purpose.

We are to be warriors, and they are part of our divine arsenal. Youth is powerful when harnessed, trained and released.

If we are to turn our hearts to the younger generation in this season and allow the Spirit of God to lay the groundwork for a move of God, then we must give time and thought to how we polish and prepare these arrows for divine work.

Firstly, let's acknowledge the theological truth that the movings of God's Spirit are for everyone, including children. When Peter stood up on the day of Pentecost to explain what was happening, as the Holy Spirit poured out on the newly formed church, he said:

*"...this is what was spoken by the prophet Joel: "'In the last days, God says, I will pour out my Spirit on all people. **Your sons and daughters will prophesy, your young men will see visions...**"* Acts 2:16-17

He continued later in Acts 2:

*"Repent and be baptized, every one of you, in the name of Jesus Christ for the forgiveness of your sins. And you will receive the gift of the Holy Spirit. **The promise is for you and your***

children…" Acts 2:38-39

It is powerful to note, that in Peter's explanation of the out-pouring of the Holy Spirit, he immediately made it clear that this was not only for mature men. No, he hit at the heart of the errors often encountered in an ancient Patriarchal society, by proclaiming this was for women and for young children too!

In other words, on the very day that the Church was birthed, children's prophetic, supernatural ministry was immediately birthed as well. I love that!

I believe this means that we should not be content with sending children out to learn bible stories, sing a few fun songs, and have them keep quiet while the adults get on with the serious business of spirituality. No, our children are able to move in the anointing of God just like the adults, and while they are infants we need to train them with that in mind.

Bring Them Into Your Tent

So how can we bring a young generation into the moving of the Holy Spirit, as promised in the book of Acts? I love these verses describing Moses having face to face encounters with God, I think they give us a good place to start:

*"Now Moses used to take a tent and pitch it outside the camp some distance away, calling it the "tent of meeting." … As Moses went into the tent, the pillar of cloud would come down and stay at the entrance, while the LORD spoke with Moses … The LORD would speak to Moses face to face, as one speaks to a friend. Then Moses would return to the camp, **but his young aide Joshua son of Nun did not leave the tent.**"*
Exodus 33:7-11

Moses would meet God in all His glory, conversing as a friend, receiving the wisdom he needed to lead. But the line that "gets me" most in this passage is the line about Joshua:

"Then Moses would return to the camp, but his young aide Joshua son of Nun did not leave the tent."

If you know your Bible then you'll know that Moses was a great leader, but it was Joshua that led the Children of Israel into the long-awaited breakthrough, finally entering the Promised Land.

Where did Joshua get the remarkable strength and boldness to enter the Promised Land? How did he succeed where Moses failed? Moses had drawn the youngster Joshua into his "Tent of Meeting" with God and then he left him there! Joshua had watched and experienced an older leader meeting God. Then he lingered in that remarkable presence and it made him one of the most powerful leaders to walk the planet.

We too, need to draw our children and youth into our places of God-encounter, if we are to raise an extraordinary generation. Giving them songs, games, moral codes and biblical principles is good, but not enough - We must give them God Himself!

I remember being around 6 years old, and one of the first worship teams in the world came to visit our church in the 1970's. Our 600 strong church must have allowed the kids to sit around the stage area, because I vividly remember sitting on the edge of the platform as they sang and worshipped, and a rich sense of God's presence invaded the auditorium. In that moment I felt God like an electricity filling me, and I knew God was more than a song, a preach, a church service or a kind principle – God was a being who loved me, wanted to know me and had reached out to me personally.

I was utterly transformed by something that was more "caught" than "taught" - I had met God for myself.

That encounter, and others that have followed, have meant more to me than all my years of Bible School training and sermons. Meeting God is deeply subjective, but profoundly life transforming. And that is what Moses gave to Joshua, and what my parents and their church gave me. They invited me into their tent, and I was transformed!

We too, need to learn how to build homes, churches and children's ministries that are places of encounter, where all generations can meet God.

The Proximity Of His Presence

When my son was about 5 years old, our church was hosting a large conference with many gathered and powerful meetings going on late into the evenings. In our household we were always pretty strict about bedtimes in those days, but we knew we wanted our son Zachary to experience the powerful presence of Jesus – to be around when God moves is unmissable, so we kept him up late to meet God.

On the Saturday evening, as I preached to the large crowd and led them into the outpouring of the Holy Spirit, my wife Victoria and son Zach were on a small balcony overlooking the auditorium. As she held him in her arms and they watched dad preach, Zach suddenly began to pray in tongues for the first time! We had sacrificially brought him to a place where he was more likely to meet God and Zach experienced his first divine encounter.

It's simple, if we bring our children and youth into the proximity of His presence, they are more likely to meet God for themselves. Nothing will change them, keep them, or envision them more!

Just last Sunday as Emily, our Children's Pastor and her team, led worship in our Revival Kids ministry, Zach, now four years older, told us that as he worshipped, he felt God reach out and touch his hands. These little, subjective encounters, transform lives, and turn religion into a dynamic personal relationship for our kids. Our Children's team has pitched a tent where God will turn up, and they've invited the children to encounter Him. They are preparing God's arrows for war!

An evangelist friend of mine took his young son to Africa, where he experienced blind eyes opening, as he began to minister alongside his dad. *"It's real dad – it's real!"* he exclaimed as he saw God move in response to his stumbling prayers! Bringing a child's heart to the realisation that *"it's real"* is vital to them walking with God powerfully, for many future years. Those who only learn bible stories, alongside our worlds Fairy Tales and endless TV shows, are more likely to fall away than those whose hearts have been touched by God's power.

I remember asking a prominent Pastor, how come his children were in ministry and walking so well with God? I'll be honest, some of them were pretty wild characters, and not quiet co-operative little things temperamentally! So, how had they turned out so powerful in God? The Pastor answered – *"Every few years a move of God would sweep through our youth and children's work, so those kids knew God wasn't a song, a game, a set of principles or a story – God was very real, very powerful and very personal. Those personal encounters held them close to God as they navigated adolescence!"*

Releasing The Arrows!

Once we have created a place of encounter and brought our children and youth into it, we need to bring them alongside us in ministry and life, with the hope that one day they will go further than us – just like Joshua ultimately took God's people further than Moses could.

This means teaching them how to worship and be filled with God's Spirit, then how to hear God's voice, prophesy, pray for each other and move in the gifts of the Spirit, as mentioned in 1 Corinthians 12. It means teaching them how God speaks through our passions and gifts. It includes showing them how to get a blueprint from heaven, gather wisdom, form a team, make a plan and go on a great adventure with God, seeing the Kingdom come. The arrows need to learn how to be released!

In one of our schools the children gathered around a 5-year-old with a broken ankle (demonstrated by an X-ray) and prayed for her healing. After the prayer she was due a second X-ray before a more permanent cast was applied for her planned six-week recovery time. Amazingly, after prayer, the break could no longer be found! The young girl took part in the school Sports Day that week.

These stories transform the atmospheres of our children's ministries and entire churches. If we bring our children alongside us and teach them how to minister, then remarkable things can begin to take place in their lives – personal memories and experiences that will never leave them.

To do all this we need to recognise that our children are not only the generation of tomorrow, but they are to be an active generation *today*. In order for one generation to arise, we sometimes wrongly think another generation has to decrease. But that is not God's way. No, he wants generations to walk and work together. Adults and children, flowing in the authority and supernatural power of heaven - that's what Acts 2 prophesies and what the *spirit of Elijah* creates!

The Sound of The Young

As well as being filled with God's Spirit, encountering His presence and being able to move in God's spiritual gifts, I also think God has given us children as secret weapons to win wars.

"From the lips of children and infants he has ordained praise, to silence the foe and avenger." Psalm 8:2

Read that again if you would – It's saying that praise and worship from children silences the enemy. That means the worship times in our kid's activities, or when we are gathered together inter-generationally, can be a powerful form of spiritual warfare! I do wonder if the devil trembles *more* at children singing than when adults do!

I believe children are meant to be part of our church weaponry today, not simply "tomorrow's generation." They are arrows in our hands Psalm 127:4-5 says. If we can mobilise our children in Spirit-filled living, perhaps a whole new sense of presence, power and purpose will open up to our churches. Perhaps new moves of miracles, of prophecy, of healing can flow, if we let them step out in their simple, innocent ways. Perhaps they'll provoke us grown-ups to jealously and get us stepping out in faith ourselves!

A friend of mine was fitting a new lightbulb in his high-ceilinged home, when he fell off the stepladder, badly injuring his back. Laying in agony he called to his five-year-old son "Get your mother!" knowing she was out of ear shot elsewhere on the property.

Instead of instantly obeying and calling for his mum, the little 5-year-old lad scurried over to his dad and did what he'd seen his dad do many times for others. He popped one hand in the air, the other on his dads injured back, lifted his little voice to heaven in praise and prayer and called out *"Jesus, please heal my daddy!"*

My friend was about to complain and correct his son when he suddenly realised all the pain had gone! He was healed!

That 5-year-old was a weapon.

We need to bring our children into our places of divine encounter, show them how to pray and how to hear God's voice and do what God says. Then we need to release them into appropriate levels of ministry, by working alongside them and releasing them to go further than we ever will. We also need to release their praises to fill our homes and sanctuaries, weaponised arrows in the steady hands of caring spiritual parents.

If we do this, we may just find we have a remarkable revival on our hands. And trust me, revival history shows that their innocent, pliable hearts have led the way in many a powerful revival. The transformation of your church, and maybe our whole land, could be sitting in those Sunday School classes of ours, if we could only start a move of God among our children.

If the Silver Surfers and the Young Arrows can begin to walk together, along with every generation in between, won't we be the most blessed of all generations?

Source
1. https://www.charismanews.com/marketplace/83738-prophetic-alert-i-am-breaking-the-age-bar-rier

JOURNAL & SESSION 8 DISCUSSION TIME

Use the questions below to ponder and journal, or to discuss this chapter with your small group or team.

1. Is anyone inspired by the thoughts of a fresh anointing for an older generation? Discuss.

2. Does your church community fully utilise the wisdom of your older generations, or have they been side-lined? How could you further release the Silver Surfers in your church?

3. Discuss honestly, the culture of intergenerational relationships in your church community. How close are the older and younger generations? Can you gauge how healthy things are among the generations?

4. In this chapter I state that the young arrows are *"meant to be in our hands, close to us. At hand."* What might this mean for your church community?

5. Similarly discuss how you might *"polish, cherish and prepare the young to be launched with purpose."*

6. The Spirit-filled ministry of children was launched on the Day of Pentecost! How could you make your children's ministry more powerful, Spirit-filled and equipping?

7. How could you bring your children into your "Tent of Meeting" so they may encounter God? It does beg the question, *"Do you have a Tent of Meeting to bring them to?"* or is that the place to begin this journey?

JOURNAL

JOURNAL

THE SOUNDS OF HEAVEN

13

The Lord says…

"With every new movement of heaven there is a sound, and this day shall be no different. From the Prayer Rooms of my House I hear a new sound arising. It is a sound of war, a sound of worship, a sound of declaration and victory – but you shall not only hear the sounds of my people as they are stirred, but also the sounds of heaven. The trumpet blasts of my purposes are being released, the mobilised angelic hosts are cheering, the joy of the whole earth is come among you! You cannot be silent my people, you must sing, you must shout, you must declare – let us do that together, you and I, heaven and earth in unison! Many worship ministries will be lifted from the human platforms of the earth, to the throne room of heaven in this coming era. Many will sing as if seeing the very face of God. Prophetic psalmists will melt the hearts of the authorities of this earth, and as I did in Jehoshaphat's day, my glory will be revealed among the praises of my people. Let your new sound arise!"

Chapter 13
The Sounds Of Heaven

"Praise and worship is such a powerful device, it is able to dismantle every shackle and it's able to breakdown every wall."
- Euginia Herlihy

Brian Taylor stated early in 2020 that *"The decade we just entered into, starting from 2020-2029 is the season of prayer or the season of the mouth, which is represented by the Hebrew letter Pey. As the season of Pey, the year 2020 and this decade emphasizes the mouth, what we speak, declare, and give voice to."*[1]

At the start of 2020, many prophets around the world were stating that this was a time of declaration, prophetic proclamation and divine decree. The *"Decade of the Mouth"* or even *"The Roaring 20's"*, some tagged it, a wonderful play on words combining the title of the exuberant, freewheeling 1920's, with the roar of the Lion of Judah! How provocative and confrontational has it has been to find many of us are legally bound to wear masks in Church and prohibited from singing during the pandemic!

Despite all this incendiary limitation, I still sense a new violent arising in the heart of the Church, reaching up with fresh, raw, prophetic worship, that covers the throne of God and our land with God's fame and deliverance. We have lingered for some time as the Church around songs of God's kindness, goodness and love, but we seem to be shifting globally towards songs of spiritual warfare, the strength of God and an emphasis on His might and power. Something is arising!

A Sound Of Worship

I believe this shift will result in a new sound in our worship in these times. A roar is being stirred, and even church leaders like me, who were historically full-time worship leaders, are sensing once again it's time to get the musical instruments out, write songs again, lead God's people in worship and let a roar of fresh heavenly praise fill our hearts and congregations! Worship leading apostles and prophets are arising in the land, preparing to usher in a new glory from heaven. Get ready!

In the US, controversial, raw, street worship and prayer has erupted in recent months. Globally, online airwaves are filled with fresh anthems, songs and sounds of praise. I believe prayer rooms and 24/7 prayer initiatives are soon to be flooded with new waves of worship too, as the Church erupts from global lockdowns as if there is *"a fire, shut up in* (her) *bones!"*

But why might praise-filled declaration be important to the birth of a new era in God? Allow me teach for a moment about the power of declaration:

The Power Of Declaration

"So God created man in his own image, in the image of God he created him" Genesis 1:27

Man has been created in the image of God and there is one powerful characteristic to God, that scripture clearly states He has included in our design too. It is a factor that plays a role in praise and worship and, under the leading of the Holy Spirit, can be a world-shaking force.

It is the power of the tongue.

In reading the account of creation, it takes very little theological training to see that God made the earth and everything in it by simply speaking. Over and over again Genesis chapter one states *"And God said…and it was"*. That was the power of God's words.

A quick leap over to the end of the Bible and in Revelation we discover that God has not changed. Three awesome descriptions of Jesus give us a pictorial view of how this power works:

"...out of his mouth came a sharp double-edged sword"
Revelation 1:16

"I will...fight against them with the sword of my mouth"
Revelation 2:16

"Out of his mouth comes a sharp double-edged sword with which to strike down the nations" Revelation 19:15

In the mouth of Jesus we find a weapon, a force and a power. That's how He spoke and created the world. That's how He healed sick people with a word, commanded demons to leave and spoke to soldiers making them fall over (John 18:6)! It is because He has a power in His mouth.

"The tongue has the power of life and death, and those who love it will eat it's fruit" Proverbs 18:21

If we are made in the image of God then it is part of our inherent make up to contain power in the words we speak. The Bible clearly states the tongue is a powerful source of life and death. With it we can bless and we can curse. Proverbs 11:11 states *"Through the blessing of the upright a city is exalted"*. That's amazing! A city's prosperity and happiness can depend on the words of blessing from the righteous.

Proverbs also states:

"The mouth of the righteous is a fountain of life" (10:11)
"With his mouth the godless destroys his neighbour" (11:9)
"The tongue of the wise brings healing" (12:18)

That is placing incredible power and influence on the words we speak.

"When we put bits into the mouths of horses to make them obey us, we can turn the whole animal. Or take ships as an example. Although they are so large and are driven by strong winds, they are steered by a very small rudder wherever the pilot wants to go. Likewise, the tongue is a small part of the body, but it makes great boasts." James 3:3-4

In the New Testament book of James, God goes a step further. He compares the tongue to the rudder of a ship. It's small, but it guides the whole ship of your life. Everywhere you go, you go because of what you have said - your tongue providing direction for your life.

From Mere Thinking To Speaking

How often do we feel embarrassed about speaking things out? I have noticed people who feel down don't often want to speak out. They want to "think about the problem". Ever been there? Of course the devil wants you to think about the problem. He wants you to analyse the mountain. To measure it. To compare it to other people's mountains. Anything but do what Jesus tells us to do with our mountainous problems:

"If anyone says to this mountain "go throw yourself in the sea" and does not doubt in his heart...it will be done for him" Mark 11:23

Don't just think about the mountain - speak to it! Move your tongue and release the weapon that God has placed in your mouth. Swing that sword, fire that machine gun, light that dynamite and level the mountain with faith in Jesus and the power He has given you to use.

Some people are obsessed about praise coming from the heart, so much so that they are afraid to let it out of their mouths. *"I'm worshipping in my heart, brother"* they say. Well *"Out of the overflow of the heart the mouth speaks!"* (Luke 6:45). God doesn't want praise to be simply in your heart. He wants the *"...praise of God to be in your MOUTH"* as well.

Spoken Praise Inflicts Vengeance

What has all this to do with praise and worship and the current heavenly stirring for a fresh warring sound, a new voice of declaration in this new Kingdom Coming era? Listen to this:

"May the praise of God be in their mouth...to inflict vengeance on the nations" Psalm 149:6

Notice the result is *"to inflict vengeance on the nations"*. Psalm 149 goes on to say it will punish, bind and carry out God's sentence against the enemy. Praise in the mouth of a believer releases the arsenal of heaven into the atmosphere around you, binding the enemy and bringing Kingdom purposes into reality where you are.

Paul and Silas were beaten up and in jail in Acts chapter 16. I'm sure they did not feel like opening their mouths. They hadn't read the end of the chapter. They didn't know what God would do in response to their praises. But they sang out and adored God in the middle of their difficulties and God's presence invaded the jail, shaking away chains and setting them free!

"Yet you are holy, enthroned on the praises of Israel." Psalm 22:3 (NLT)

You see, the power of God rides on the praises of His people. He somehow infects every faith filled word with His authority, bringing all His Kingdom's resources to bear in a situation. As we open our mouths in worship, the same Kingdom and glory that is invading our hearts at God's throne invades the spiritual heavenlies around us. As we confess His Lordship, pray under His inspiration, with singing and rejoicing, all God's Kingdom comes to earth. As we release our tongues to declare the wonders and Lordship of Christ, the powers and principalities around us experience the same world creating, devil commanding, sickness destroying power that God has in His own mouth, the very mouth that made the universe!

Announcing In The Heavenlies

"His intent was that now, through the Church, the manifold wisdom of God should be made known to the rulers and authorities in the heavenly realms." Ephesians 3:10-11

Here the apostle Paul shows us that one role of the Church is to make God's wisdom known in the heavenlies. The heavenlies are the invisible realms of power and authority across the earth, made by God but often occupied or influenced by evil forces (Ephesians 6:12).

Paul says it's your job and mine to declare God's purpose to them. How do we do that? Through our mouths of course! Through proclamation, praise, declaration, preaching, worship, prophecy, the public reading of scripture, teaching and prayer. These all decree God's authority and purpose to invisible realms, preparing the ground for God to move and the Kingdom to come.

That's exactly why He teaches us to pray and say *"Your kingdom come, your will be done, on earth as it is in heaven"* (Matthew 6:10).

Church, let the sound of your praise, prophecy and proclamation fill your church buildings, the airwaves, your homes, your streets and the heavenlies over your nations. As you do God's purposes will be released like they were for Paul and Silas (Acts 16). God's deliverance will erupt like it did for Jehoshaphat (2 Chronicles 20). God will be enthroned as it promises in Psalm 22:3 and the praises of our children will silence the enemy as it assures in Psalm 8:2. Pathways of purpose will be prepared, new eras announced, fresh ways opened, and season changes proclaimed. Mountains will move, heavenly powers will heed His decree, and the sound will precede the coming of the Glory of the Lord, as was experienced in 2 Chronicles 5.

"The trumpeters and musicians joined in unison to give praise and thanks to the LORD. Accompanied by trumpets, cymbals and other instruments, the singers raised their voices in praise to the LORD and sang:
"He is good;
   his love endures forever."
Then the temple of the LORD was filled with the cloud, and the priests could not perform their service because of the cloud, for the glory of the LORD filled the temple of God." 2 Chronicles 5:13-14

The Sounds Of Heaven

Not only is the sound of our proclamation and praise to be heard in this season, ushering in new encounters of glory and new days of strength, there is another sound found in the pages of scripture and revival history that I believe is being released in the earth right now.

My friend Andrew Murray (Not the dead one, or the tennis player, but rather the outstanding revivalist on our staff!) has recently written a timely and prophetic book called *"The Sound of Heaven"* – I highly recommend it if you want to go deeper into this theme.(2)

In it he speaks of the new sounds of worship, of revival, of prayer, and of praise about to be released in the earth. Now the sounds of worship and praise are easy for us to understand, but there is also a mysterious sound from God that is about to be released among us I believe.

I have heard the sound of heaven myself several times in my life. Some call it the "sound of revival" – a certain extra something, like a sound within the sound, or the echoes of a distant and glorious realm approaching.

One of the first times I heard this sound was on a trip to Mexico in the 1990s, where I was singing, the guest of a gathering of 6,000 leaders, who were obviously in some state of revival and renewal as a movement. Something much more than the notes I played, or the melodies I sang, invaded that auditorium, and for hour after hour, for several days, thousands of leaders lay weeping, worshipping and at times wailing like Isaiah in God's temple (See Isaiah 6), as the sound within the sound swirled through the crowd, and the rushing winds of heaven landed among us.

In more recent times I heard it again. A church full of young people from Scotland were visiting a nearby revival centre where I was preaching. Before I spoke our host asked the youth group to sing a worship song for us. As the sweet, fresh faced Scots began to sing, I heard again, the sound within the sound. Heaven was in the notes. The fear of God visited that room. Many wept, while many others could not move.

Just last year I found myself speaking at a great annual convention for a church denomination in Spain. The larger meetings were good, but quite normal, with passionate, healthy worship and bold preaching. But then I was asked to speak to around 200 youth leaders. I shared about intimacy with God and revival for a short while and then we prayed. Once again, without any musical manipulations, something engulfed the group, and through the tears of worship and longing, I once again heard the distinct sound within the sound – the sound of revival, as heaven and humanity fused together for a moment in divine prayer.

More than just the infusion of a worship-sound with a remarkable new depth or dimension, sometimes we can even literally hear audible sounds made by God Himself! I am part of a global network of prophetic creatives called Sounds of the Nations, and our leader and founder, Dan McCollam tells of the time he was involved in leading worship in the 1990's. As the worship leader sang the word "fire" in spontaneous praise and prayer, a sound like a ram's horn blasted through the sanctuary from the heavens. Every time the worship leader sang "fire" the supernatural sound would echo it – to the amazement of all gathered! I have seen the videos of this event and it is quite remarkable and astonishing, just like Acts chapter 2!

Don't be shocked, there is plenty of biblical precedent for the sounds of heaven being heard on earth. Acts 2:2 states *"Suddenly a sound like the blowing of a violent wind came from heaven and filled the whole house where they were sitting."* Israel heard heavens trumpets (Hebrew 12:19), Adam *"heard the sound of the LORD God walking in the garden in the cool of the day"* (Genesis 3:8) and some even heard the audible thunder of God's voice in Jesus day! (John 12:29). These supernatural occurrences appear varied and common place during days of the visitations of God.

A newspaper headline during the days of the Welsh Revival proclaimed *"Something from another world is at work in Wales"* – That was over 100 years ago, but the sounds of revival from heaven are still stirring our souls to prepare for the coming glory of the Lord.

I believe the sound of revival is being released upon the earth as we enter this new era. God is releasing a new rhythm for our times. And those who hear it, those who echo it, those who metaphorically dance to it, will see God's Kingdom come to earth in glory.

By the time the 7th and final trumpet sounds in the heavens we know that *"the kingdoms of this world"* will have become *"the kingdoms of our God"* (Revelation 11:15). The Church will be revived. Society will be transformed. Ultimately everything will be renewed. And *"the earth will be filled with the knowledge of the glory of the Lord, as the waters cover the sea."* (Habakkuk 2:14).

He is coming – and we must learn to listen for His Sound, that we may sing and proclaim with Him, and dance with Him into incredible days of glory.

Sources
1. https://godtv.com/the-decade-of-the-mouth-is-upon-us
2. https://www.amazon.co.uk/dp/B083KHYM75/ref=dp-kindle-redirect?_encoding=UTF8&btkr=1

JOURNAL & SESSION 9 DISCUSSION TIME

Use the questions below to ponder and journal, or to discuss this chapter with your small group or team.

1. What might it mean for us to be in a season of *"the mouth"* – of declaration, proclamation, praise and prophecy?

2. How could your church release a greater sound of praise in the coming months?

3. How could you further invest in your worship team and their own skills and vision?

4. Does anything need to change in your services, to give more time to prophetic proclamation?

5. How often do you train your entire church congregation how to worship, praise, pray and prophesy? Regular development in this area delivers vibrant results for most church cultures. How could you develop your congregational worship culture more?

6. Has anyone ever heard any supernatural sounds of heaven? Tell your stories.

7. Why not take some time to pray, praise and proclaim right now, and let the fresh sounds of worship fill you and your team.

JOURNAL

JOURNAL

Chapter 14
The Church Has Left The Building

"God would not send a problem your way, without provision attached to it!"- Graham Cooke

During the unusual Divine Reset birthed in 2020, the song of the year was a declaration called "The Blessing" from Elevation Church. The song was subsequently rerecorded and released by many worship leaders in many nations around the world.

It is a confession of faith and truth that we need to hold close as we venture into the uncharted territory of a new era. Its lyrics state:

"The Lord bless you and keep you,
Make His face shine upon you and be gracious to you.
The Lord turn His face toward you and give you peace.
May His favour be upon you,
And a thousand generations,
And your family and your children,
And their children and their children.
May His presence go before you,
And behind you and beside you,
All around you and within you,
He is with you, He is with you.

In the morning, in the evening,
In your coming, and your going,
In your weeping, and rejoicing,
He is for you, He is for you."[1]

As the song ends it crescendos with a repeated climactic finale singing lines like *"He is with you"* and *"He is for you"* driving home the revelation that we are not left alone with an unknown future ahead of us.

It would seem *"I will be with you"* is God's most common answer to any question in the Bible, and *"I am for you"* comes in at a close second. He is on your side. He is not against you, has no plans to harm you, and is working daily for your development and blessing. Doesn't that pretty well solve every issue we will ever face? If God is for us, what could ever defeat us!

Another song of the season comes from Brazil, where popular videos of prayer and intercession on the streets of that beautiful nation during the 2020 pandemic lockdowns, feature alongside the old Pentecostal spiritual, sung in Portuguese of course:

"Because He lives, I can face tomorrow,
Because He lives, all fear is gone,
Because I know who holds the future,
My life is worth the living just because He lives."(2)

As we stride forward, sailing across this unfamiliar ocean of promise and adventure before us, we must remember that God's love and wisdom reaches beyond every horizon that beckons us. God stands in every tomorrow summoning us forward like a parent teaching a child to walk. He solves every problem before we even encounter it!

"God would not send a problem your way, without provision attached to it!" Graham Cooke

What a thought! As God is good and *"works everything together for our good,"* (Romans 8:28) we must conclude that everything He allows, from Pandemics to daily problems, He will only use to perfect, grow, strengthen us and show us further grace, while deepening our intimate knowledge of Him and His love for us.

As we near the end of this time of preparing our hearts, homes, families and churches for the new era ahead, knowing that *"He holds tomorrow"* should transform how we face the future. It gives us faith and hope, that God will use every problem to show us the greatness of God and grow us into the image of Christ. Begin to see that every problem, *even when **not** sent by God Himself,* can be turned into an opportunity to know Him better, grow more Christ-like, and grasp His grace more deeply.

Let me leave you with a few final prophetic encouragements God has given me during this remarkable Reset time. I hope they leave you comforted and reassured just a little more as I conclude.

"Slow Down"

One thing God has said to me again and again this year is "Slow Down" – in fact, He usually says it VERY slowly. *"Stop rushing, stop being so needy, stop hankering for more, and start to live in the moment"* is what I sense Him say.

I must admit, I'm often in a terrible rush, and He's really been driving it out of me this year. It's as though I often live spinning my wheels in such haste. And God says *"Slow down and let your tyre tread go deep. You'll actually go faster if you do!"*

Slow down to go faster. Mmmmm…there's a God idea in that I think.

"It's Not About Failing, It's About Unveiling"

The next thing God said so clearly to me this year is that this troubling, difficult time, with tricky decisions, frustrating complexities and daunting challenges, is that He's not brought us to this place to fail.

On Sunday 9th February 2020, without any inclination of what the year would hold, God said to me through a dream, *"I've not brought you here to fail, I've brought you here to be unveiled."*

I think this time will be for our good and for the making of us all. It will clarify our callings, unveil true identities, sharpen our focus, and develop a bold confidence regarding our destinies. Like Shadrach, Meshach and Abednego (Daniel 3), we will find that this fiery trial is actually burning the limitations off us all, like the ropes in that fiery furnace! The fires will release us from doubts, reticence and fear. Many are being delivered from delay and deliberation. Chains are falling away. Ropes are being burned. Locks are being undone and divine doors opened. LIMITATIONS ARE BEING LOOSED! Expect to come through this time more confident, settled, mature and ready for all God has for you. This time will be for your unveiling.

"The Church Has Left The Building"

On the night of 14th December 2020 I had a dream. In the dream I was leading a church service from the stage, with many in attendance. As I was about to announce the guest speaker, hundreds began to leave the service from the rear of the hall. Rapidly, they streamed out in droves, leaving the building virtually empty!

"What's going on?!" I turned and asked another leader on the platform, exasperated and confused.

"They want to go out now and preach the Gospel on the streets!" came the reply.

In the dream my heart filled with a mix of frustration regarding our redundant plans for the service, including our now pointless guest speaker! But I also felt genuine joy that something of an uprising of desperation to share the gospel was driving the church in multitudes out of "my service" and onto the streets to share the Gospel!

As I woke the words *"The Church Has Left The Building"* filled my mind, at the vivid scene of hundreds of church goers exiting the service.

I believe God has been using the unusual events of 2020 and beyond to cause the Church to "Leave the Building." He has been releasing us from our old ways of building-centred programmes and our propensity to place the value of "gathering" above the value of "going" in our western, consumerist, modern church cultures. He is prising the fingers of many leaders from old ways and methods with a violent grace!

Multitudes no longer content to attend a good church, listen to sermons and enjoy sing-a-longs, are going to rise up with a desperation for the "Real Thing" found in the Book of Acts – a longing to share the Gospel with signs following, to fight for justice, to feed the poor and visit the prisoner, to bind up the broken hearted and set free the captives. To live vibrantly in a pioneering adventure with the Holy Spirit. The Church is leaving the building to build the Kingdom!

New innovative ideas from heaven for outreaches, businesses, influential forums and new church projects will flood the ranks of the Church. For some it will almost seem like a rebellion against the religious norms of the last 50 years, as it will be an uprising from the congregation, but not always from the normal platforms of leadership. In fact, there will be places where the leadership are doing all they can to return to normal church life, post-Coronavirus, yet the people will want to rise to a faith that is more radical, more original, more like the early Church, with its escapades, energy, fruitfulness and dangerous passion.

In some places the people will ignore the leaders (as the crowd ignored me on stage in the dream!), and head off with God, such will be the *"fire shut up in their bones"* to shift up a gear in God's purposes. A "Righteous Rebellion" against religious form will drive many from the meeting place to the market-place, finding new, innovative, fresh ways to infiltrate the world with the Word, and usher in the Kingdom.

Church leaders must be willing in this time to give up the frustration that all is not as it was, and even that our attempts to return to normal are continually thwarted. Instead, we must give way to the smile in our hearts of the uprising of God's people! Successful, godly leaders will be the ones who give way to the new longings for a deeper prayer-life & God-encounter among us. Sunday services alone won't do – we must go deeper.

They would also be wise to give way to a new spirit of unity and collaboration that will almost seem so extremely selfless, it threatens the very concept of the success of your "own" church, in preference for loving, serving and working with others. This will deeply challenge the egos of many leaders.

Finally, leaders must also give way to the drive to the harvest field that will rise up in church members. *"We must do more for the poor, for justice, to speak out, to reach the lost, to heal the hurting,"* will be the heart cry of many in the pews. *"Less playing at church, much more Kingdom Come!"*

Leader, give way to the shifting purposes of heaven. Give way to an uprising of passion for the lost. Give way to the call for collaboration. Smile as your own plans are thwarted by an uprising from heaven stealing the agenda. If you do, you will find the favour of God and the joy of a true shepherd will fill your heart.

While there will always be a godly place for gathering as the Church, may the era ahead be the time the Church left the entrapment of our building centred programmes, to *"Go into all the world"* as our Master commanded!

Embraced By The Man Of Fire

Finally, some months ago, while seeking God for fresh strategies and wisdom to navigate this Divine Reset, I dreamt I met the Holy Spirit. In the dream He appeared like a Man of Fire to me. If you've ever seen a movie stunt man set alight in a fire-retardant suit, it was pretty similar! However, He wasn't staggering around in agony, He was walking towards me with purpose, peace, confidence and grace.

Embracing me with His burning arms and drawing my head to rest on His blazing chest, He gently answered my longings for strategic wisdom for the future.

"This is the strategy," He quietly and firmly whispered, *"This is the strategy."*

Slowly the hot flames of His heart began to ignite the dry places of my own soul. Electricity pulsated through my chest, the bubbling hot lava of heaven stirred in my heart, excitement, passion, energy and strength simmered in my soul.

"This is the strategy," He continued to whisper, as flames poured from His strong embrace into my entire being, *"This is*

the strategy."

To be hugged by the burning passion, love and energy of heaven – sometimes that is all the strategy you need! To be saturated again in the power and presence of God, to be enveloped and overwhelmed by the raging rivers of His grace and to fall overwhelmed, into a fresh all-engulfing baptism of the Holy Spirit, that is what will be truly era-defining.

God's Spirit, poured out upon us from Acts chapter 2 onwards, is often pictured as a *"fire"* throughout the New Testament (Matthew 3:11-12, Luke 3:16-17, Acts 2:3-4, 1 Thessalonians 5:19).

Daily I have meditated on the burning embrace of the Holy Spirit and the cold, tired embers of my weary heart have been rekindled again, stirring the flames of wisdom in me, with which I write this book to you. I have written, not to encourage in you an endless pursuit for new, clever or complex ideas, but rather with the desire that the new fire that is shut up in my bones, would burn in you too. That we would end our time together so engulfed in the fires of His embrace, and that there we would find all the wisdom we need, as His voice leads us and His power energizes us.

Let the Man of Fire embrace you right now. Sit back in the burning arms of your Comforter and Counsellor and listen humbly for His voice. If you do, you will have all you need to face the future.

Sources
1. Written by Steven Furtick, Chris Brown, Kari Jobe, Cody Carnes © 2020 Music by Elevation Worship Publishing, Capitol CMG Paragon / Writers Roof Publishing, Worship Together Music / Kari Jobe Carnes Music
2. "Because He Lives" is a song by Bill Gaither / Gloria L Gaither

JOURNAL & SESSION 10 DISCUSSION TIME

Use the questions below to ponder and journal, or to discuss this chapter with your small group or team.

1. *"God would not send a problem your way, without provision attached to it!"* says Graham Cooke. Discuss how this statement can bring you comfort for any area of lack you currently face.

2. God often tells me to *"Slow Down!"* – Does anyone else need to hear this right now? How might we encourage each other to choose a healthy pace for life? What are the things in your own lives that cause you to feel you need to rush?

3. In the dream I've called *"The Church Has Left The Building"*, the congregation streamed out of the building, desperate to give themselves to a higher task, *preaching the Gospel*. How might this idea be expressed in your own life/church culture? Where does the idea of simply being scattered and disorganised have its limits?

4. What have been the most pertinent lessons, challenges and changes you will make from reading and discussing The Divine Reset?

5. The Holy Spirit is like a *Man of Fire!* End your time together today, by inviting the Holy Spirit to embrace you and fill you, and take time to entrust yourself to His counsel and power, for the exciting era ahead. God is with you!

JOURNAL

JOURNAL

EPILOGUE

As I close, let me leave with you some phrases that sum up all I feel God is saying for us as we enter this new day. This, I truly believe, is God's plan, intention and longing for us as His Church.

As you read, read slowly, and let the prophetic potential of a glorious Bride arising in the earth flood your heart with the purposes of Jesus.

I dream of a Church filled with God's magnificent glory.
Her members are adventurers, not mere attenders.
Her leaders are releasers, not containers; equippers, not superstars.
Her children are powerful, not merely baby-sat or redundant.
Her youth are leaders, strong in word, purity and deed.
Her attitude is Kingdom, not self-preservation or self-promotion.
Her heart is generous, giving until it hurts, preferring others beyond themselves.
Her worship is passionate and filled with encounter, not mere song singing.
Her prayers are fervent, not apathetic; they are effective & authoritative, not empty.
Her influence transforms nations, politics, laws, businesses, medicine, education, the arts, the media, morality and the family.
She innovates, with fresh ideas and strategies to transform the world.
She leads, she does not follow.
She amplifies the message of the Gospel.
She clarifies Christ's call to discipleship.
She exemplifies the unmatched love of God.
She is filled with miracles, signs, wonders, healings, deliverance and joy.
Her services are presence filled, powerful, challenging and Je-

sus focussed.
She is clean & clear, in a world of moral filth and confusion.
She is gracious to the hurting & sin-bound – everything she touches is made clean.
Her Lord is JESUS, her power is of the SPIRIT, her love is of the FATHER.

THIS is the Church I'm dreaming of.

JOIN OUR TRIBE

If you are inspired by the ministry of Jarrod and Victoria Cooper and want to stay connected, why not join our online community of passionate learners, leaders and churches across the world, dedicated to growing in God, growing in skills for life and leadership and growing in God's presence and power for revival.

There are currently three levels of Tribe membership:

Tier 1 – LEARN (Access to our growing online digital library)
Tier 2 – LEAD: Global Leadership Tribe (or GLT for short.)
Tier 3 – LEAD+ (Group access for up to 10 leaders)

Membership includes:

- Unlimited access to all our online courses and extensive library of video and audio teachings.
- Free books
- Private webinars, teaching series and online coaching sessions.
- Private Facebook group to interact closely with Jarrod, Vicky and other tribe members.

**Visit JarrodCooper.net/join-our-tribe
for more information**

Download Our FREE App

NEED SPIRITUAL INSPIRATION?

Are you feeling uninspired spiritually? Need a fresh daily devotional? Are you ready to move beyond the stress, anxiety, and weariness of this rollercoaster year? Are you looking for fresh clarity and confidence in God for the years ahead? Do you want to connect with people who are prophetic, with a proven 30-year track-record in lifting, inspiring and bringing hope and faith to lives, and releasing people into fresh God-encounters?

We have good news for you! Jarrod & Victoria Cooper's new, free, TRIBE app will bring you:

- Daily faith filled devotionals
- Teaching broadcasts
- Prophetic words
- Worship
- Podcasts
- Regular Livestreamed events

All FREE OF CHARGE to your app, with the ability to upgrade your subscription to the global online learning community and team mentoring tiers of THE TRIBE if desired – but no pressure, just enjoy the free stuff above by all means!

Simply download the app to your smartphone today and start being inspired straight away!

Head to JarrodCooper.net/app or scan this QR code with your smartphone to download.

About Jarrod Cooper

Jarrod is an author, songwriter, broadcaster & communicator, and is privileged to lead Revive Church in Hull & East Yorkshire.

Inspirational in style, he uses speech, song, worship and prophetic ministry, in an inspiring, challenging and humorous way to encourage the Church to reach higher in God. This work has taken him throughout the UK, Europe, Africa and the Americas since 1990, speaking at churches, conferences, on television and radio and through writing and producing training and coaching materials.

His main passion is that "the glory of the Lord would cover the earth, as the waters cover the sea", and seeks to lift believers to a life in the supernatural, that will display God's presence and power in everyday life.

Jarrod has been involved in producing over twenty albums, including eleven solo albums, and the song he is probably most known for writing, King of kings, Majesty has featured consistently for over a decade, as one of the top 10 worship songs sung in the United Kingdom (CCLI). His weekly radio & TV teaching programs REVIVE and Days of Wonder broadcast in many nations weekly and he has authored several books, including "500: Are we entering a new era of glory?" – "Stronger" – "When Spirit & Word Collide" and "Glory in the Church".

Revive Church is presence filled, prophetic, pioneering and passionate and is fast becoming an apostolic resource centre for leaders, for training, for missions, for church planting and inspiring revival. Revive Church is the home of Colombia Child-Care UK, a ministry birthed by the remarkable David Taylor, which educates, feeds, bring medical care and the Gospel to over 1500 children every week.

Jarrod is married to Victoria and they have one young son, Zachary.

Books by Jarrod:
Believe & Confess Group Discussion Guide - 2020
The Multi-Site Church Adventure – 2019
The Leadership Quest, Volume 1 – 2019
Revive Stories – Inspiring Stories of God at Work Among the People of Revive Church in Hull & East Yorkshire – 2019
Stronger – The 40 day Devotional – 2018
500: The beginning of a new Church Age – September 2017
Believe and Confess (with Victoria Cooper) – August 2017
Stronger: building a powerful interior world – 2016
When Spirit And Word Collide – 2015
Glory in the Church – 2005

Albums by Jarrod:
Lost in Your Glory – 2017
Sanctuary (1990-2015) – 2016
Dreaming – 2015
Shine on Me – 2015
Beautiful River – 2006
King of kings, Majesty – 2004
Rend the Heavens – 2002
I Tremble – 1999
Days of Wonder – 1998
Song of the Bow – 1996
Deep Calls to Deep – 1994

Follow Jarrod on:
YouTube: youtube.com/jarrodlcoopertv
Facebook: facebook.com/jarrodlcooper
Instagram: @jarrodlcooper
Twitter: @jarrodlcooper

For resources, blogs, news, podcasts and much more visit:
JarrodCooper.net